Now in her mid-eighties Gilda Frantz shares with us what she has learned from life and from being a Jungian analyst. She has written a feeling, intuitive wise woman's shorter version of her own *Memories, Dreams, Reflections*. Personal insights links essays on subjects drawn from her life and work, there is poignancy and an affirmation of indomitable spirit in her musings. She knows firsthand about difficult childhoods, early widowhood, aging, death of a beloved grandchild, and closeness to the end of life. She knows about suffering and the creativity and soul growth that can go hand in hand. These are themes in her own life and in her observations of others. *Sea Glass* is an apt metaphor for this book—to discover why requires reading it.

—Jean Shinoda Bolen, M.D., author of *Goddesses in Everywoman, Goddesses in Older Women*, and *Close to the Bone.*

You could be listening to the storyteller by the fire, or to your favorite aunt at the kitchen table—the one who always makes you laugh—so vital and engaging is the narrative voice in *Sea Glass*. In fact, you are reading the gathered writings of Gilda Frantz, a beloved Jungian elder in the classical tradition. Frantz is on intimate terms with the gods and their myths. She has personal experience of alchemy, individuation, dreams, and the creative process, all of which she describes in accessible and lively language. *Sea Glass* sparkles with gems, including Frantz's interview with the film director Fellini and her amplification of the story of Pinocchio. Like the sea glass for which she names her book, Frantz has had a difficult life, been thrown about on waves of fortune, battered on the rocks of childhood poverty, parental divorce, early widowhood, and the death of a son and granddaughter. Her wit and wisdom has been polished to a fine glow. She is eloquent in her reflections on the meaning of suffering. *Sea Glass* is most luminous when addressing the toughest topics—loneliness, grief, abandonment, aging, and death. It is a comfort and an inspiration—strong medicine for the soul.

—Naomi Ruth Lowinsky, author of *The Sister from Below: When the Muse Gets Her Way* and *The Motherline: Every Woman's Journey to Find Her Female Roots.*

Sea Glass

A JUNGIAN ANALYST'S EXPLORATION OF SUFFERING AND INDIVIDUATION

Gilda Frantz

Sea Glass
A Jungian Analyst's Exploration of Suffering and Individuation
Copyright © 2014 by Gilda Frantz
First Edition
ISBN 978-1-77169-020-1 Paperback
ISBN 978-1-77169-021-8 eBook

Published simultaneously in Canada, the United Kingdom, and the United States of America by Fisher King Press. For information on obtaining permission for use of material from this work, submit a written request to:

permissions@fisherkingpress.com

Fisher King Press
www.fisherkingpress.com
+1-831-238-7799

Many thanks to all who have directly or indirectly provided permission to quote their works. Every effort has been made to trace all copyright holders; however, if any have been overlooked, the author will be pleased to make the necessary arrangements at the first opportunity. See pages 215 - 216 for a list of contributing individuals and organizations.

Book design by iWigWam
www.iwigwam.com

Front cover image *Looking Out* © is from an original collage by Marlene Frantz.
www.marlenefrantz.com

DEDICATION

To my daughter, Marlene Frantz, a generous, kind, and conscious woman, who is an important part of everything I do and brings me joy and happiness.

ACKNOWLEDGMENTS

Many thanks to . . .

Marlene Frantz, who generously loaned me the use of her collage for the book's cover. She encourages her children and her friends to do their own thing, and she did the same for me.

My editor and muse, Margaret Ryan, who helped birth this book and is always there for me.

Char Marie Sieg, who can do anything and never says "I can't." She helped me see the book as a reality.

Michael Gellert, author and Jungian analyst, who took me under his author's wing and generously gave me so many useful ideas.

To all the people who sought me out to be their therapist, I say thank you for also being my teacher and adding to my understanding and greater compassion for suffering.

Caroline Davis, who provided expert reference investigation services.

Lynda Becker, my wonderful bookkeeper with whom I've been close friends for over 30 years.

Norma Gillett, a fine nurse and caregiver.

Katie Sanford, who inspired me by publishing her first book at 89.

My many colleagues at the C.G. Jung Institutes in Los Angeles and San Francisco for their affection and friendship these many years.

Stephen Martin, Jungian analyst, co-founder of the Philemon Foundation, who invited me to become a board member to join in helping Jung's *Red Book* see the light of day.

Julie Sgarzi, Marlene Frantz, Rachelle Elias, and Patricia Amrhein, our *Red Book* reading circle that was enriching.

Peter Levitt, poet, teacher, and friend, who said it was a great idea.

Jay Scully, my trainer, who helped me to become physically strong.

My mother, Ruth Gersten Feldrais Striplin, who gave me the gift of generosity.

My sister, the late Joan Feldrais Burman Langford, who taught me to read at age four and opened a window to the world of books.

My late half-brother Hank Feldrais and my loving half-sister Penny Haberman, who were and are my good friends.

The late William O. Walcott and Albert Kreinheder, who helped me become a better writer by inviting me to assist at the beginning of *Psychological Perspectives* so long ago.

My artist friend, Nancy Mozur, who inspires by always being who she is.

My last analyst, Bernardino Zanini, who brought me back to life in old age and helped me regain the ability to be creative again.

Max Zeller, Hilde Kirsch, James Kirsch, Edward Edinger, C.A. Meier, and my other Jungian analysts and teachers, to whom I will always feel deeply grateful.

My colleagues, Glenn Foy and S. Robert Moradi, who appreciated my writing.

My grandchildren, Ariel, Kieffer, Zalman, and Malka Katz, who brought me a new life as their grandma.

My late husband Kieffer, who was and is my everything.

To my late son Carl, whom I miss daily.

My nieces and nephews, Franz, Frantz, Burman, and Haberman; to Mike and Amrita Franz and Lin Burman Bixby I give special mention.

And lastly, thanks to Mel Mathews, an exceptional human being who took a chance on me and opened the door and invited me in.

CONTENTS

PREFACE

I have been fascinated with sea glass ever since I was a little child growing up one block from the Atlantic Ocean. When we moved to California, we lived near the Pacific Ocean, and in both locations I became familiar with sea glass. As a child I had no way of knowing that these gem-like stones were originally broken shards of bottle glass that somehow wound up in the ocean. I'm pretty sure the glass is first a bottle or some very thick glass so that it can endure the beating it takes in the roiling sea. Were they wine bottles tossed over the side of an ocean liner plowing the wine-dark sea? Were they once carriers with a message a lonely person wrote on a desolate island in the middle of nowhere? Broken glass doesn't hold messages except as a metaphor. Once the glass was a vessel and now it is only a piece of what it once was.

Who knows how long this process takes? From broken pieces of glass they become small, simple shapes to hold in one's hand and feel the silk-like texture of the gem. When the realization dawns on one of how sea glass began as a clear, broken shard of bottle glass, it is amazing to see what it had to go through to become so delicate and beautiful. It made me think of what a diamond has to undergo to become a priceless gem: great pressure in the earth, formed from carbon after eons of time, it becomes a luminous stone once the outer covering is removed and the stone undergoes polishing. It made me think of what humans go through in life . . . what I've gone through.

When I was casting about for a title for my book, the image of a piece of sea glass came to me. It dawned on me that the process the glass endures in the ocean is not dissimilar to what happens psychologically when a person is wounded, broken, and goes through life's capricious twists and turns. We either drown in the sea, or if we can get a foothold, possibly our fate changes and we can begin to grow consciously from the nightmare we have suffered. Or maybe our fate doesn't change at all.

Individuation is a process of growth and a movement toward becoming a whole person. As much as I can discern about this innate process, a person encounters profound suffering, begins to ask questions about why his or her life is like this, and then finds a way to gradually begin to understand that this road of suffering can lead to greater meaning, a greater deepening in the soul. Think of a wounded soldier whose legs are blown off in battle. The adjustment to this new state does not happen overnight. It sometimes takes a long time for the ego to understand that we are still a whole person even if we need artificial limbs in order to stand. Occasionally the person who suffers amputation was an athlete and finds the strength to ski again on artificial limbs. We all think of this person as a hero, forgetting that there are other people who made incredible growth leaps, not by heroically skiing but by writing or painting or just living each day.

Now imagine this: You are seeing me as an 86-year-old woman. It is midday. I am in my bedroom having a nap, and I am dreaming:

> *"Why don't you do something good for yourself,"* an inner masculine voice says to me. I sit bolt upright in my reclining chair. In a split second, I am on my feet and in a trance, sort of like sleepwalking. I stand up and go into my living room, down two steps, directly to a certain bookcase . . . and begin taking books off the shelf and putting them on the coffee table nearby. I open each book, see that there is a chapter or article in it written by me, and put it on the growing stack of books.

After looking at every book and journal and creating several piles, I begin to come out of the trance. I sit down and begin to count the number of pages I have written and am amazed that they number over 300. I look at every article, surprised that I have forgotten some of them. It dawns on me that these books contain *my* collected works—and there are dozens of other papers and articles stored in a box in my office closet or garage. So it isn't all the writing I've done, but it is the writing that has been seen by a mere handful of readers of the journal I helped found in 1969 and those readers who follow Jung and Jungians.

Still in a kind of rapturous mood, I reach for the phone and call two friends, one, the Senior Editor of *Psychological Perspectives* whom I respect a lot, and the other, an individual who can do anything and who was the Managing Editor of *Psychological Perspectives* throughout the 1990s. I trust these two women and ask each if she will help me put together a book of my writings, a memoir of sorts. Each says the same thing: "Absolutely."

By the time the phone calls are completed, I sit quietly, now fully awake, and remember a dream I'd had in April 2006, about seven years before, when I was 80. It is important that I tell that dream here because it is the beginning of everything to do with this book. I need to add that I had always wanted to write a book and even began a novel, when I was in my 20s, about three young adventurous women. Being young, I lacked the discipline to rewrite it and to see if it was publishable, so it is now yellowing somewhere with other orphan writings. Another issue that kept me from writing a book is the misapprehension that I, as the writer, am supposed to do everything by myself—not just the writing but EVERYTHING else. That idea always defeated me. Thus, it was startling that I called on my two helpers while in that trance, asked for assistance, and got it from two powerful women who know their business.

Now to the other dream.

April is my favorite time of the year, not just for the beauty of nature coming to life after a long winter, but because it is the month in which I married my late husband. Even though he's been gone a long time now, I still cherish the memory of our courtship and wedding in April of 1950. April is also the year I traveled by myself as a little girl on a Greyhound bus from Chicago to Santa Monica. I arrived on April 14, 1934.

Back to 2006. Easter was coming, and although I am Jewish, being married to a non-Jew brought Christian holidays into my life and, conversely, made me more aware of being Jewish. I happily participated in Easter, as my husband joined in my Jewish holidays. The night of my dream I'd had Passover dinner with a dear friend who is an Orthodox Jew. I love the retelling of the Passover stories and went home with a light heart. I soon went to bed, fell asleep, and had this dream:

I hear a man's voice say to me, "You are not a good landlady." I am shocked and feel indignant, which shows in my reply: "That's not true! I am a good landlady. I saved the life of a neighbor who needed a place to stay—I rented my guesthouse and took her to the hospital when she became ill. I even stayed with her in the ER. How does that make me a bad landlady?" His reply, in his sonorous voice, shocked me: "You don't take care of your own property."

I grew quiet and just stood in front of the Voice thinking back to another time. In my memory, I was making a plan for my old-old age. I arrived at the conclusion that I could rent out my home and occupy the small house in back, which was designed as a guesthouse and was adorable and cozy. I had built it for my friends' use when they visited Southern California. I lived a block or two from the beautiful Pacific Ocean. My home was on a rustic street with a huge sycamore tree growing in the center of it. It was a picturesque canyon and a nature-filled place to live.

When I awoke, I lay in bed replaying the dream in my mind. I knew that the unconscious was talking to me directly, and it sounded like a kind of warning. I wondered how it would be to live in the back guesthouse and have people living in my home. What if I didn't examine their monetary fitness carefully enough to assure myself that they could pay such a high rent, and what if the renters *didn't* pay the rent? I'd had that experience a few years before, when I inherited a condo from my son and rented it (albeit unconsciously) to a con artist who didn't pay the rent! After months and a lot of red tape I had to evict him—and what a pain that was. I asked myself: What if I was dependent on that money and it wasn't being paid?

In my heart I knew that the amplification I was adding to the dream was only a part of how the dream might be viewed, because dreams are often layered in terms of meaning, but the idea of renting my house and not being paid grabbed hold of me and I knew exactly what I had to do. A couple of weeks later I had a vision that my next-door neighbors might buy my home, and by this time I knew the worth of the property and offered it to them. My daughter knew just the right person to help me with the complexities of selling a house, and she connected me with a realtor. In less than three weeks I had sold my home, and my fate was set on a particular course. The dream kept coming into my thoughts, but I didn't really do any more work on it, even with the lingering feeling that there was much more to the dream.

Moving was fateful. Due to my daughter's belief in the dream, she kept me from buying just any "dump," as I so colorfully labeled the houses I had seen, and she said, and I quote, "God wouldn't have sent you this dream to have you move into a dump. Just keep looking." That very weekend I found the place I call Brigadoon. It is a little over 8 acres of tree-filled gardens surrounding beautifully designed townhomes that are not crowding one another. Its presence is a well-kept secret in Santa Monica. Synchronicity played a huge part in my finding it, and I bought the perfect unit and that was that. Or was it?

The dream about "doing something good for myself" brought the true meaning of the first dream into the foreground. I had neglected my creative work by not giving it the respect it deserved. All creative work deserves a place of honor in our lives; my papers were languishing in a box, collecting dust, many not read or seen by anyone. An analyst writer, the late Jack Sanford, once remarked that the Muse doesn't like it if we store HER inspirations in a bedroom drawer. She feels these papers and articles, or paintings and poems or whatever the creations, are intended to be seen and enjoyed by many, not just a few.

My body actively participated in realizing the meaning of the "doing something good" dream. I didn't just wake up, I stood up and walked to where the answer was waiting for me. I felt moved in my body to follow my heart and soul to the destination of my life. I've been writing since I was about 9 or 10 years old and can recall the first story I wrote, while waiting for a bus, about ants going to and fro a little hole in the ground.

These two life-shaping dreams were about my creativity. Finally, I found the impetus to bring my papers together and to see that they tell the story of my life as well as explore basic human themes: abandonment, living with loss and grief, the meaning of loneliness, and the beauty and challenge of aging.

I've been a Jungian analyst since 1977 and continue to practice at age 87. I know there is much this book will offer to those wrestling with the same issues—archetypal issues that everyone faces sooner or later.

Thank God for dreams.

Gilda Frantz, Santa Monica
April, 2014

I loved the old man
who touched my
life with outstretched
hand
and left his
mark
upon my soul.

—Gilda Frantz[1]

---

1 Gilda Frantz, "I Loved the Old Man," in *C.G. Jung, Emma Jung, and Toni Wolff: A Collection of Remembrances.*

Part 1

ARCHETYPAL SUFFERING

What is it, in the end, that induces a man to go his own way and to rise out of unconscious identity with the mass as out of a swathing mist? Not necessity, for necessity comes to many, and they all take refuge in convention. Not moral decision, for nine times out of ten we decide for convention likewise. What is it, then, that inexorably tips the scales in favour of the *extra-ordinary*? It is what is commonly called *vocation*: an irrational factor that destines a man to emancipate himself from the herd and from its well-worn paths. True personality is always a vocation and puts its trust in it as in God, despite its being, as the ordinary man would say, only a personal feeling. But vocation acts like a law of God from which there is no escape. The fact that many a man who goes his own way ends in ruin means nothing to one who has a vocation. He *must* obey his own law, as if it were a daemon whispering to him of new and wonderful paths. Anyone with a vocation hears the voice of the inner man: he is *called*.

—C.G. Jung[2]

---

2   C.G. Jung, "The Development of Personality," CW 17, ¶ 175. Note: CW refers throughout this publication to the *Collected Works of C.G. Jung.*

Chapter 1

THE GREYHOUND PATH TO INDIVIDUATION

Originally published in
Marked By Fire: Stories of the Jungian Way[3]

I have always identified with those Jews whose fate it was during the Holocaust to either have to flee their homeland with what little they could carry, or to be jammed into boxcars and sent off to endure the horror of murders, starvation, and illness in the death camps. As a child born of Jewish parents, I had a frequent fantasy that I could get past Hitler's guards and sneak into his secret hideout and kill him. In my fantasy I didn't know how I would do this, only that somehow a little girl like me might get close enough to Hitler to kill him. I wanted to save my people.

At an earlier time, I worried about the poor of the world and created a solitary game in which I was a scientist who was trying to invent the perfect food that would end starvation throughout the world. It was made of a pinch of cereal and some other types of dry food that I would grind into a powder with a mortar and pestle. In the fantasy play, one pinch of this concoction would end world hunger. I felt very powerful in this fantasy/play, and whenever I was left alone (which was often), I would enter my "laboratory" to grind the cereal into a powdery substance and see in my imagination a starving child being fed just a little of this—and poof!—his or her hunger would cease. In modern Jungian parlance, I felt like an alchemist.

---

3 Gilda Frantz, "The Greyhound Path to Individuation," in *Marked By Fire: Stories of the Jungian Way*, 38-46.

When my mother was in her seventh month of pregnancy with me, on a certain cold winter evening, my parents had an explosive argument, which culminated in my mother's leaving her beautiful home. She woke up my 11-year-old sister and walked out into a stormy, freezing, eastern seaboard night. She obviously expected my father to follow her and bring her back to warmth and safety, but he never did. This event marked both her fate and my sister's and my own fate to wander, gypsy-like, from New York to California.

Jung wrote that as long as children were connected to their parents, they had to suffer the fate of those parents. But when the children grew up and left their parents' home, then they could discover their own destiny. And that is what happened to me.

I grew up feeling that my father was despicable for what he did to my mother, sister, and me by not being there when I was born and seemingly not giving a damn for any of us. His lack of any kind of support forced my mother to be the sole provider for the three of us. As I grew up, I became the conduit mother used as the means to try to get my father to support us. I would call him and ask for money for my mother, but it never worked. We were in the Great Depression and it was almost impossible for my father, a designer of very fine women's millinery, to obtain employment. He didn't support us at all, so my mother had to find ways to put a roof over our heads and food on the table. She worked in so many different jobs: baby nurse, cook in an elementary school cafeteria, cook at a dude ranch, sewing at a WPA factory that made workingmen's clothes. She was a woman of classic, natural beauty and possessed a very lively sense of humor and a wild imagination. She even saw herself as an inventor and, indeed, she invented a lost key service, as well as a way to use the remnants of colored bar soap to make a bubble bath concoction (this was before there was such a thing as bubble bath). Neither of these inventions brought her anything material, although Western Union was interested briefly in the key service, but she enjoyed the creative process involved in their conception and production.

Our instability caused us to move a lot, possibly as often as once every few months. When things were tough and no money was coming in from her jobs, we'd move "just to change our luck," as Mother put it.

I went to so many elementary schools I lost count; I never stayed long in any of the schools. We never were hungry, thankfully, as my mother was always able to feed us. She had the gift to make everything seem like an adventure, so life was not bleak growing up, though it was rootless. I said to my analyst once that I'd never had a childhood, but she disagreed and replied, "You had a childhood, you just didn't have the one you would have wanted." And that is the truth.

In the summer of 1938, I was 11 years old and being tossed back and forth, like a potato *latke*, between my mother in California and my father on the East Coast. My older sister had married the year before, so now there was just my mom and me, which for me was very sad. My mother was still working at whatever job she could find, and I was alone a lot. Also, by that age I was beginning to do what my mother called "develop." My "developing" worried my mother so much that even though we loved one another, she was tossing me back to my father. One morning she told me, "You are going to live with your father, the rat; I can't take care of you anymore."

And then she went on and on about how he never supported us and that the strain and responsibility, now that I was "developing," was just too hard. As I translated her words, developing really meant "becoming a woman"—and becoming a woman scared me to death because when I got my period, the first words out of my mother's mouth were an anguished, "Ugh, my god, now you are a woman." I wanted to cry because from my vantage point, being a woman was a kind of hell. My mother worried all the time, worked as hard as she could all the time, and as far as I could see, didn't have much of a life. And her breasts hung down to her waist, for which she blamed me. Evidently I nursed her ravenously as an infant, and her pendulous breasts were the result.

I had lived with my father for about 6 months when I was 10½. I was a tall, slender child with long dark-blond hair, large hazel eyes, and a rosy complexion. I looked about 15, but if you heard me talk you would know I was a much younger child. I was intelligent and pretty, but still I was a child. My father didn't know me very well due to my having been raised solely by my mother, but he liked well-mannered pretty children and was proud of me. When I lived with him he made me tell my school chums that my mother was in a sanitarium for her "health." I never knew if he meant a sanitarium for tuberculosis or an insane asylum. Being divorced somehow shamed my dad, and he didn't want the school to know that my parents were divorced.

I missed my mother and got lonesome for my sister and her little girl, so my father eventually sent me back to my mother and now, less than a year later, she was doing something very irrational. Her plan, as she outlined it to me, was to send me by Greyhound bus to New York City, informing my father at the last moment, by Western Union, that I was coming. She said I was leaving the very next morning and she already had a ticket—a child's ticket. This meant I would have to let her bind my little breasts, wear a childish dress, and wear my hair in pigtails so I wouldn't look my age.

I like potato latkes a lot. I love the smell of a latke frying in chicken fat, and I love to hear the sizzling sound the fat makes. With applesauce and sour cream on the side I could eat a lot of latkes, but being like a latke in hot fat didn't appeal to me—in fact, I hated it. As was usual in my life I had no time to say anything to any of my friends, as it was summer and we were all scattered. Because times were so tough, I doubt that many went to summer camp or on vacation, but they did have grandparents who lived on farms or in other towns, and they could visit them and have fun. I had no such luck and was simply reading even more than usual and mostly staying in the room my mom rented with a view of Sunset Boulevard in the Echo Park area.

The next morning my mother put me on a bus, a label pinned on me saying who I was, and we kissed tearfully goodbye. I watched her disappear as the bus pulled away and off we went.

A tired latke child arrived after five days on the road at the station in New York City and saw my father standing there scowling, waiting for the bus door to open. He had on his overcoat and a brown fedora. The wind was blowing, and it was getting cold outside. I was stylishly dressed—though for a younger child—in a coat, hat, and gloves. As I walked down the steps to hug him, he said sternly, "Your mother is crazy. I am married and you cannot live with me." I was always a quiet child not given to tantrums or yelling, but at that moment I wanted to scream. I wanted my mother. Before I knew it, we were walking up the steep stairs to the elevated and waiting for a train. I just went with him; I didn't cry noticeably or make a fuss. Sitting on the train in the Bronx I heard the story. He received the telegram, which came to his home, so he had to tell his "new" wife that he had been married before and had a child. (He still didn't tell her about my older sister.) She had a fit and (as my father told the story) pulled at her hair, screaming, "She can't live here! What will my family think of my marrying an older man who had been married before and has a family?" She had married my father after a short courtship, and he had never told her his right age or that he had children—nothing.

I heard only part of what he was saying as I blindly tried to think of a way to escape from him somehow. I felt such hatred and loathing for him, I could hardly look at him. "We're here," he said and took my hand. As the train door closed behind us, I screamed, "My purse, I left it on the seat!" But it was too late, the train was pulling away and my leather handbag and all I had in the world went with it. Then my tears flowed, and I began to feel sorry for myself and for the mess I was in.

We arrived at a house—a huge-looking three-story house on a tree-shaded street. We walked up the stairs to the front door wordlessly. At the sound of the bell, a woman appeared at the door and gestured us to come in. The little *latke* had found a home.

As luck would have it, it turned out to be a real home, and the people were all good people. I actually enjoyed living there after getting over the shock of being unceremoniously dropped into a strange environment. The occupants were Orthodox German Jews, all Holocaust survivors, and it was at their dinner table that my outrage of what was happening in Germany was ignited. One Sabbath, I sat next to a newly arrived couple, a man and his wife who had escaped from a concentration camp and were now in New York—the tattooed numbers on their arms very visible. They were both very thin, so thin I could see the woman's facial muscles jump and move as she chewed. I listened to them speaking German, and slowly I began to learn German, which was a little like the Yiddish I had learned as a child. Although I had forgotten much of the Yiddish, some of it still came back to me, and in no time I could eavesdrop on conversations to my heart's delight. I learned enough to hate Hitler, and I began having my fantasies of saving the Jews of Germany by killing Hitler.

I stayed in this home happily for about six months. Dutifully I wrote my mother, telling how I missed her, how awful the people were where I lived, but that my father, the rat, didn't care; that he visited me only once a week for about an hour and then gave me a nickel when he left. I told her that I was doing well in school and had made friends, but that she was my beloved mommy and I hoped to see her again. I had not completely forgotten how impulsively she had sent me away on a day's notice, and I knew I was torturing her by telling her how unhappy I was. Well, my clever little plan backfired:

One cold spring morning, the lady of the house awakened me, telling me that my mother was downstairs and that I should dress quickly and come down. I was in shock. Mother, *here*? She had come to "rescue" me from my unhappiness—and off we went to another place, another adventure. Not long after that I wrote to my sister in California and asked her if I could live with her and help her with her baby, who by then was a year old. She gave her consent, so back I went, alone again on the Greyhound bus, this time heading west across the country. My mother stayed in New York. Living with my sister and her little family was a rich experience that gave me the understanding I needed later in life when I became an analyst. In fact, it would be easy to say that my entire early life gave me what I needed in ways that are difficult to write about.

When I was in my early twenties, I met a handsome prince and was carried off into the land of Jung and Jungian analysts. He was older than I, and of a different religion, but neither of those differences mattered because we were both deeply in love. When I learned how old he was, I thought, "Well, I certainly still have a father complex." I had often dated older men, so being in love with an older man made me realize that I still had one. I read a lot and was very interested in psychology. (In high school I diagnosed my mother with having delusions of grandeur, which was how I described her to my English teacher.)

After my prince and I became engaged, I began to realize that my future husband had two families, one of his birth and one comprised of Jungian analysts, both colleagues and teachers. Thus, my two sets of in-laws were familial and collegial. Before I met his *family*, I met his Jungian analytic friends and teachers. The colleagues looked me over carefully, but I was accepted and hugged and embraced by his birth family. It took me years to feel accepted by the colleagues and for me to accept them, but overnight I loved his birth family and they, me.

I was 23 and the Los Angeles analysts were probably 25 years older than I, or more. I think I dressed the way many young American women dressed when they were about to meet people important to their betrothed. However, my youthful and stylish presentation stood out rather blatantly amid the conservative, sturdy gray wool suits the analysts and their wives wore. The founders of the Los Angeles Jungian community were all refugees of Hitler's plan to murder millions of Jews. They wore what they brought from Europe and had the look of the intellectuals I had met as a child when my mother went to communist meetings and brought me with her. I observed these intellectuals and found them strange and fascinating. I was 8 or 9 years old. The women let hair grow under their arms and on their legs, and the men didn't shave their beards or cut their hair, so much that they looked scruffy. The analysts didn't look scruffy, however. In fact, there was an elegance to their appearance. They just didn't look like Americans.

As a bride-to-be, I found it ironic that I'd had warm and comfortable feelings for German Jews and other refugees since childhood, but with the refugee analysts I found it particularly hard to feel that I was myself in their company. It was only years later that I learned one of them had actually been in a concentration camp and the others were simply conservative and from another generation, let alone another world. Eventually I did become close with all of them, and loved them, but it took work on all our parts. I know they didn't get behind my persona to see the real me.

My fiancé's way of introducing me to his analytical colleagues and teachers was to bring me to a lecture given by Max Zeller, a kind, gentle soul who spoke with a thick *"ziss und zat"* Berlin accent. I could not understand a word that he said (he had not been in this country that long). On top of that, I had no idea what his topic was about. While I had heard about Freud and knew a little about his theories, Jung was totally a mystery to me. I had never attended such an event before, and I had never before been introduced to a group of people as someone's fiancée. I dressed to the nines for this lecture, wearing a very pretty suit and a tiny hat with a feather, a large feather, that went from the back of the hat and stuck up in front. The hat was a tiny saucer-like shape and the feather was the most outstanding feature. I also wore wrist-length gloves and carried a chic handbag. (Everything matched, as this was 1950.) I thought I looked lovely, but to my shock, I looked so conspicuously overdressed next to the practical outfits worn by the women. In addition, the women all had short, bobbed hair, whereas mine was long and wavy and a golden reddish blond. Not only was I overdressed by everyone else's standards, I also *fell fast asleep* during the talk. Dr. Zeller droned on and on in his thickly accented English, and his words became more and more impossible to understand; against my will sleep overtook me. It was as if Morpheus had intentionally sprinkled sleep dust over my head. I fought sleep, biting my inner cheek and digging my fingernails into my flesh, but it was a losing battle.

Meanwhile, the feather fluttered through the air as my bobbing head betrayed my state. I woke up at the end of the lecture to the sound of polite applause. I quickly gathered my wits to compose myself and shake hands, smiling and nodding, happy to meet all of the people whom my fiancé wanted me to meet.

One woman, the wife of a soon-to-be analyst, tormented me for the next thirty years by telling that story of first meeting me, with that hat with the feather that bobbed as I napped, and how funny it was to her. That she lived a long life is through no doing of mine, because for years I thought I would strangle her each time she told the story to a gathering. Finally, I relaxed and began to see the humor, and just like I am now doing, I too began to tell that story and enjoy the laughter it produced.

One would think with this beginning that I would turn away from Jungian analysis, but I didn't. I went into analysis—with Dr. Zeller! He was a sweet man, and together we dealt with all my adolescent insecurities. After Dr. Zeller, I took time off to have two babies and then was ready for more analysis. I worked with Hilde Kirsch and learned more and more about Jung and how I might, one day, become more conscious. I wrote my dreams down faithfully, did active imagination, drew my dreams, and in general spent a lot of time working on understanding my unconscious and my shadow.

Many, many years later, widowed by then, I was in Zürich on business about the film *Matter of Heart*, which was being shown to the Swiss Jungian community. I met many of Jung's closest followers, and his son Franz Jung, at a party at the Institute after the film was shown.

Since I was to be in Zurich for a week I decided to have what James and Hilde Kirsch had told me about—something known as the *Zürich Experience*. This experience occurred when an American came to Zürich for analysis and stayed for a month, seeing an analyst daily for the entire time, while immersed in dreams, drawings, and writing. I was to be there only a week, but I had something on my mind that might just lend itself to an "instant" analysis. I chose to go to C.A. "Fredy" Meier, who was brilliant, handsome, virile-looking man. Dr. Meier was puffing on his ever-present pipe when I came to his office. We sat down and were silent for a few moments, giving me a chance to gather my thoughts and take in his office. It was small, cozy, and filled with books and manuscripts he obviously wanted to read, stacked all over the room with beautiful rocks or stones on them to keep them from blowing away.

When he asked why I was in his office, I burst into tears and told him about my terrible inferiority complex around my difficulty with thinking.

"Yah?" he said, reaching into a nearby drawer and handing me a sheaf of papers. "You must take this test, and we will find out about your thinking." And so away I went back to my pension to take a typology test. When I returned a day or two later, Dr. Fredy used a special form to determine my typology by my answers. He puffed on his pipe and then looked at me over the glasses perched on his nose and said, "Gilda, your intuition and feeling are off the chart, maybe one hundred or more, but your thinking and sensation are both three." And looking at me with a delighted look in his eyes, he shouted, "You CAN'T THINK! You shouldn't have a complex since your thinking function is *really* inferior!"

I instantly felt better, and could then move on to some of my dreams. I left Zürich so impressed with this vital man who was so alive and had such a healing effect on me. His last words to me as I went out the door at our last meeting were: "Do research! Jung would have wanted Jungians to do research." And off I went to continue my journey, feeling somehow that I had been initiated into the larger Jungian world with this meeting. Fredy Meier is no longer alive, nor are any of the first-generation analysts. There are now at least three training institutes in Zürich, probably two in Italy, and so on and so forth.

I miss those old days and all those people who became part of my family. My daughter Marlene and son Carl thought of James and Hilde Kirsch as their grandparents, Max and Lore Zeller as their beloved aunt and uncle, and the Zeller children felt like older cousins to them. I too literally grew up in this Jungian environment and found my destiny in their midst.

I am now in my mid-eighties and have been an analyst for almost forty years. The memories I have shared belong to the dusty, distant past, yet they also have a life of their own. My life's journey is a splendid example of luck, love, and individuation, but it is especially one of fulfilling my destiny.

Chapter 2

GROWING UP POOR IN LOS ANGELES

Originally published in *Psychological Perspectives*[4]

When I was in India in 1981, I was stunned by the extreme poverty and starvation I saw on the streets of Calcutta. In planning this trip I experienced some trepidation about the poverty I knew I would encounter, and I wondered whether I would be able to take in the suffering. Seeing families sleeping in huge reclaimed oil cans on the streets of Calcutta and begging for food for their babies was very difficult, and inwardly I felt grateful that we did not have those conditions in Los Angeles. While eating in the dining room at the Ramakrishna study center where I was staying, heavy velvet drapes were pulled so that those on the street could not watch us eat. It was hard to swallow food, knowing that just beyond those drapes were hungry people.

Within months of my return to Los Angeles, however, I began to notice changes. When I took my early morning walks, I saw that men were now sleeping in the park near my home. I saw them standing on street corners begging for a little money to buy food.

In the intervening years, these conditions not only have not improved, they have worsened. Nevertheless, it is so easy to avoid seeing the grinding poverty in L.A. The poverty is softened by a backdrop of the natural beauty of mountains, beaches, and deserts. Everything looks so good, particularly if you stay on the Westside. In order to see great deprivation, you have to travel to the eastside. Even on the Westside, however,

---

4   Gilda Frantz. "Growing Up Poor in Los Angeles: A Memoir," *Psychological Perspectives* 48(1), (2005): 25-36.

there are beggars, panhandlers, and bag men and women, pushing their overstuffed carts hung with full plastic bags, looking very much like caricatures of consumerism.

In this article, I want to give you a direct experience of what it was like to be poor in Los Angeles in the 1930s from a child's perspective. First, in this car-centered city it is hard to visualize how few automobiles were on the streets of Los Angeles in these years. Because of severely depressed economic conditions, very few people owned a car. Public transportation was so good that cars were considered luxuries and were used mostly for pleasure on weekends. Thus the term "Sunday driver" was coined to describe a bad driver. People would take friends and family, stuff them to a large sedan, and drive to outlying areas that eventually became our suburbs. There were no freeways. The valley was a place of orange groves and ranches. We brought food for a picnic on those occasions.

The population in the 1930s was around 2 million people in L.A. county; now there are almost 10 million. I recall sitting in a classroom and hearing that the population of the United States in 1936 was just under 130 million. So the problems of overpopulation did not exist yet, though at least 200,000 migrants came to L.A. during the Depression. They were met at the California border by police with drawn guns telling them to go home, that California did not want them. Fortunately they got across the border with the help of the ACLU. In the 1930s the devastating dust storms in the Midwest forced sharecroppers and farmers to abandon their farms, and piling their old jalopies with family members and personal possessions, they drove west. They believed the romantic depictions of California in the movies and came to get their share of the wealth that was so obviously accessible out here. The climate beckoned, and the agriculture did too.

The city of Los Angeles looked like a postcard illustration: palm trees, the city hall standing where it is now, surrounded by nothing but clear blue skies. There were warm sunny days and only occasional catastrophes such as floods and earthquakes.

People walked everywhere, and everyone was on the move all the time. As a child we walked from midtown to downtown L.A. on a nice

Sunday, and a walk of 4 or 5 miles was not unusual. There were few service stations and very little fast food available. There really was no destination on these walks-just to see the city was reason enough. Most people did not lock their doors at night, and it felt safe go out no matter where you were. Racial prejudice and segregation did exist, however. Still, the idea of gated communities was not yet a reality, so there was an openness to the city. The beaches were uncrowded and the pier in Ocean Park, which no longer exists, was a really fun place. Dance contests were held there and old people played checkers in the sun.

For the most part, telling the truth was valued highly and was expected. In spite of the poverty, people were essentially honest in their dealings. The adage that children were seen but not heard was current thinking, but they were not really seen either. The era of the child had not yet dawned. Life felt simple. What drove people were the necessities of life and how to acquire them; food, jobs, and housing. Some who had no money for food would go down to the pier in Santa Monica and ask commercial fishermen for fish; they usually got one or two. This is how people survived, by their wits and their courage.

My story is that I was a poor child, cared for by a mother and teenage sister. We were part of a vast migration for survival that was taking place in the 1930s, activated by the Great Depression. We did not know about the avalanche of people who were descending upon California and Los Angeles in particular. Thousands were streaming into Los Angeles seeking warmth and jobs and the fulfillment of their dreams. Many were running from the catastrophic dust storms in the Midwest, and some, like my mother, simply felt they had to leave the lack of work in the East and go West toward warmth and the possibility of success.

My mother believed the movies and the myth. She came from the East Coast to avoid the cold as well as the gloom that pervaded the area since the stock market crash of 1929. In New York City over 5,000 people were selling apples in the streets. I was sent to live with her brother and his wife while she and my sister went ahead to L.A. I did not yet know about the Great Depression (I was not quite 6 years old), although I had seen signs. When people would visit my aunt and uncle, they often asked my uncle for money. And he always gave them something.

(Once he gave my mother a suitcase full of IOUs from people who owed him money, and said it would be hers if she could collect. Of course, she couldn't.) My aunt and uncle had the appearance of being well-off: fine clothes, a grand piano, beautiful home furnishings. My aunt had jewels and furs and gowns. They had a house and maid and a laundress. I was sent to join my mother on the West Coast just before they lost their home and their stores because of the terrible economic conditions. When I visited them in 1939 they were living in a small apartment. They told me that they kept their money under the carpet in the living room. Ten years after the crash, they still did not trust savings banks.

Being an imaginative woman, a poet by nature and not very well grounded, but with a great sense of adventure, my mother came West by limousine. She answered an ad placed by a limo driver and learned that for a pittance she could be driven to L.A. with other people, by the driver who had to deliver this limo to the studios. He placed the ad because he hoped to make a little extra money out of the trip. My mother and sister arrived in L.A. and found a tiny guest house in Santa Monica and planned for my arrival.

It was a bold move on my mother's part because she knew no one in this city and had no real education or preparation for what lay ahead of her. She was driven by her separation from my father and the need to support herself and my sister and me. If we became ill we went to the county hospital. There was no hospital or medical insurance for anyone, and the poor especially had no net in the event of illness. Just like today. My mother did not have a formal education but was well read, loved classical music and theater, and was somehow able to use her personal charm and intelligence to find work and support us, albeit meagerly. My teenage sister also worked at small jobs that brought in very little. She also attended Frank Wiggins Trade School to learn more about design. Mostly we worried about making ends meet—or as Mother put it, "keeping the wolf from the door."

Children who grew up in the 1930s were the real witnesses to the adult struggle to find food, work, and shelter.

My mother headed initially to the beach area believing, like other migrants, that what she saw in the movies really existed: that millionaires and movie stars befriended poor people, took them in and helped them become rich. She believed in miracles. The movie *My Man Godfrey*, starring William Powell and Carole Lombard, best exemplifies her perspective. The story is about a starving homeless man (Powell) who is found in a hobo jungle by a very beautiful and wealthy young woman (Lombard). He is her prize in a scavenger hunt. She drags him home, wins the prize at the party, and he somehow becomes the family butler. Of course the wealthy girl and he fall in love at the end and he teaches her and her family about the dignity and fellowship that can accompany poverty. That he is a very well-educated and cultured man made the transformation intriguing to watch, but my mother and millions of others believed the make-believe of being plucked off the streets into great wealth.

My mother came to L.A. not merely *hoping* to find fame and fortune, especially for my older sister, but *expecting* to find it. My sister was 17 and very pretty. She, too, dreamed of being "discovered," which meant she wanted to become a movie star. She resembled the glamorous movie stars of that time and had a sweetness and innocence that was the image of the ideal "girl" in the 1930s. I have a vivid memory of her dressed in a pair of powder-blue riding pants (similar to those worn by Cecil B. DeMille) and a matching man-tailored powder-blue shirt that had tiny embroidered flowers on the collar. Her jodhpur boots were highly polished, and she carried a riding crop in her hand. She had never been on a horse, but this felt to her like an outfit a movie star might wear to take a walk. That was the illusion—that just around the corner a producer might come walking and see her on the street and hire her for his next starring role opposite Cary Grant or Leslie Howard. Other than a gift for costume design, my sister had no training or skills.

When I was 10, my mother bought me a party dress. I had not had a party dress since I was 3 years old. Before the Great Depression all my clothing was custom-made by my father's sisters, who were in the children's custom clothing field. They worked for designers or designed the clothes themselves. Smocking, those tiny tucks in material that was done by hand and very expensive, was the rage in little girls dresses, and I had many of these. However, I had long outgrown them. When I lived with my aunt and uncle, my aunt bought me many dresses with matching panties and hair bows. But that was years ago, too. I think my father was coming to Los Angeles to see me for the first time in years, so my mother bought me a dress that, like my sister's English riding outfit, was more costume than dress. I was very tall for my age, and slender; I have a snapshot of myself in this dress. Pompoms around the pink skirt made it flare out when I walked. I had a little matching sweater that also had these pompoms (golf-ball sized) around the cuffs of the sleeves, and a matching hat. I looked adorable, but resembled someone out of the Nutcracker Suite.

People at that time were very kind to older women (my mother was 36) with children. I think they understood what a struggle women like my mother were having. Today one rarely offers a hand to the less fortunate. There was a civility during the Depression in Los Angeles. It was a time when people gave up their seat on a streetcar for an older person or helped them across the street. Women were treated in a courtly manner, and courtesy was taken for granted.

The Depression created a situation in which everyone was in the same boat. Nine million bank accounts were wiped out overnight by the crash of October 29, 1929, and people lost every cent they had. No one was immune to the shock of loss of money and status. The amount of bank failures and homes lost humbled everyone. And jobs like the bank accounts, disappeared overnight. In the recently published allegorical novel, *Life of Pi*, the teenage hero finds himself in a rowboat on the ocean with a full-grown Bengal tiger. The reader's constant question is, how can he survive this? In a way the Depression in Los Angeles was like that. Poverty was the tiger, and we, the poor, were the teenage boy. For us the danger was that poverty would attack our spirit and destroy us.

If I were to be asked what was the biggest difference between then and now, it would be that poor people were treated with a little dignity. Perhaps not much, but some. Courtesy, manners, dignity, and integrity all meant a lot in the 1930s, especially if you were poor.

Hollywood Boulevard then was a clean, glamorous, and dignified place where the well-to-do and movie stars shopped. It was a destination for shoppers who had money. There were no graffiti, no rubbish on the streets, just beautiful shops.

There were breadlines and soup kitchens in L.A., but I do not remember them on Hollywood Boulevard. The young men in L.A., restless and unable to find work, often enlisted in the CCC, a conservation corps set up by the Roosevelt administration. These young men did all sorts of important work such as building roads and planting trees; even more importantly, they were kept off the streets and out of trouble. They were given a little pay, food, shelter and clothing.

There was a tent city on Sunset Boulevard in Hollywood near Western Avenue. Tent cities were springing up all over the country and were derisively called *Hoovervilles*. Usually these Hoovervilles were situated near places where crop pickers congregated, but this one was in the middle of L.A. There was a hobby shop at the corner owned by Reginald Denny, a movie star. My mother had befriended a poor woman with a daughter around my age, and we went to visit and bring some soup. The tents were built on wooden platforms and had facilities that were shared by the residents. A covered walkway connected the tents to an office or facilities, so that in the event of rain residents stayed reasonably dry. There was a heater in the tent we visited and it felt warm and cozy to me. I have no idea who built these tents or how much it cost, if anything, to live there. The daughter of my mother's friend grew up to become a bona fide movie and TV star with her own show, called *Pete and Gladys*. The myth of L.A. became reality in their case.

Work was scarce and my mother had to invent ways to find work and care for us. She was a survivor, so we never starved or went hungry, but we ate very cheap, albeit nourishing food. My mother was able to make anything taste good—things like liver and baked beef heart. She was a warm, fun, caring, generous woman who would give food or money to a total stranger if they seemed worse off than we were. She taught me generosity on a daily basis, and I still cannot pass a poor person without offering something to him or her. All my friends know this habit and groan when I reach into my purse. I would rather give money to the wrong person than take a chance on passing someone who is desperate and hungry.

We lived all over L.A., from the beach to mid-city to downtown. We always lived in what were then nice residential neighborhoods. The area around Western Avenue and Santa Monica Boulevard was such an area, populated by immigrants from Eastern Europe and markets and butcher stores that sold kosher meat. Echo Park, another residential area, was home to many followers of a Christian cult led by Aimee Semple McPherson who built a temple there and led a mystical Christian ministry. In Ocean Park not far from where beautiful hotels now stand, a small house on a tiny lot a block from the beach could be purchased for $500. I did not know anyone who could make that purchase. There was wealth in Los Angeles—I just never saw it.

Orange trees grew everywhere, so that the city smelled like orange blossoms. Avocados were called alligator pears and were considered exotic. The air was balmy and soft blue skies with puffs of clouds made walking to and from school enjoyable.

Many children were latchkey children. Occasionally I was too. I would came home from school and wait for my mother to get home. Being protective, she often warned me not to turn on the stove and not to let in strangers. I remember often playing alone in the kitchen and fantasizing that I was a chemist, "inventing" an alchemical mixture of grains and cereals which I ground up into a powder. I thought I had invented a perfect food, only a pinch of which could cure world hunger. I also played with kids on the block and read a lot. If there was a library nearby, I would read everything in the children's section. We had very few toys, and many children made their own. I used my imagination and entertained myself. I began writing stories, and by the time I was 9, I kept a diary of secret dreams and hopes.

By age 10, I had evaluated our situation psychologically and decided that my mother was immature, unpredictable, and impulsive, because to my young observing and very judgmental eye, she did not seem to learn from her mistakes. What I was unable to comprehend then was that our little family was caught in a collective disaster beyond anyone's comprehension and way beyond my mother's ability to know what to do. It is only in later life that I realized that my mother was powerless to do much to change her situation, because the panic and depression were very deep and existed worldwide. The Depression did not end until America went to war in 1941. It took the magnitude of a world war to do what individuals were helpless to accomplish: namely, to provide employment.

Being poor was made to seem like an adventure by my mother. She believed in both luck and magic. Nevertheless, it was a tremendous struggle for all of us. We were on welfare, given food stamps, and literally supported by the Roosevelt administration. My mother worked by the grace of agencies who helped people like us. Getting on welfare was not hard in those days. I think people were believed when they said they had nothing. Everything we owned could fill three shopping bags.

If you ever have an opportunity to do so, visit a welfare office and take in the atmosphere. I dropped by one in West L.A. recently. The clerks sit behind a thick, clear shield intended to protect them from the welfare applicants. An armed guard stands outside near the door to be called if there is any kind of dispute. The welfare applicants are angry, sullen, and desperate. It is not a place anyone would choose to be.

My mother never learned to drive and we never owned a car, nor did we have a phone. At the time only one family out of every eight in Los Angeles had a telephone. I was 13 before I had a bike. Los Angeles welfare gave a needy family of five $10 a week for food, $25 a month for rent (only if they were desperate) and $5 for incidentals.

My mother always sought work. She took care of newborn babies and their mothers while I was cared for by my sister. Mother cooked in school cafeteria and sewed clothes in a factory. In the summer of 1936 my mother and sister went to Salinas to pick lettuce. I read recently that in 1936 the lettuce growers were hiring people who would work for pennies (less than a dollar a day), such as Chinese, Filipino, and Mexican workers who were imported to pick lettuce, thus bypassing the farmers and sharecroppers who fled Arkansas and Oklahoma during the dustbowl storms. The growers would advertise for 200 pickers at 2¢ a head of lettuce. When 1,000 showed up, the lettuce growers lowered the pay to 1¢ a head knowing they had all the advantage. Thus the pay was less than a dollar a day. However, if two people were able to make $12 or $13 per week between them, that was pretty good money in those days. While my sister and my mother picked lettuce, I stayed with family friends on their farm that summer near Salinas and had the best time hanging out with all the children and animals and eating the great food the farmer's wife cooked. A true city girl, I drank warm milk straight from the cow and delighted in the new, earthy smells of hay and newly mown grass.

In the 1930s children did not dress the way kids do today—meaning, they did not follow fad or fashion, because they did not choose their own clothes. Clothing was practical and meant to last as long as possible; hems were let out and shoe leather was cut when dresses and shoes were outgrown. All of America was suffering and the children suffered, too. Here is a letter from a child to Eleanor Roosevelt, which touchingly describes this suffering.

Pineville, N.Y. April 20, 1935

Dear Mrs. Roosevelt,

I am writing to you for some of your old spoiled dresses if you have any. I am a poor girl, who has to stay out of school on account of dresses and slips, and a coat. I am in the seventh grade in school but I have to stay out of school because I have no books or clothes to wear. I am in need of dresses and a coat very bad.

A little boy wrote Mrs. Roosevelt that Santa did not come to his house that Christmas. His mother told him Santa could not because they had no chimney, so he and his brothers and sisters awoke to no presents. He felt terrible shame while back at school after Christmas vacation, having to listen to children telling about what gifts they had received. He told Mrs. Roosevelt that he had heard that she cared about children and, please, could she could send his family something. Consider these headlines from 1932:

- U.S. Steel lays off another 10,000
- Chicago teachers feed 11,000 children
- General Motors Stock down from $500 a share to $10
- Suits and coats for $15

- 110 children in NYC die from malnutrition
- Business failures 1929–1932: 85,000
- Weekly income of a stenographer: 1929—$45; 1932—$16
- Banks: 1929–1932: 9,000 failures and 9,000,000 accounts wiped out.

During the Depression the majority of people were poor. There were degrees of poverty, to be sure, but everyone was humbled. Today, the split between rich and poor is much wider. Some children wear $100 running shoes, while others have no shoes or wear shoes that are hand-me-downs. The kids who wrote to Mrs. Roosevelt have no one to write to today, unless it is a TV or movie star who is known to be compassionate. Our current administrations in Washington and in California do not seem to care about the disadvantaged. The Roosevelt administration, whatever else its flaws might have been, cared and showed it by helping the poor and less fortunate people in this country.

The poor today in Los Angeles have a much harder time than we did in the 1930s. Single moms on welfare in Los Angeles have it so much worse than in 1934. The children of 2004 are saturated by TV ads telling them they have to buy this or have that. The pressure on the poor is enormous. In the 1930s one did not need rental history to rent a room because the homeowner, dealing with their own fears about losing their home, had to rent out rooms, so they did not ask. Men and women today cannot obtain work without references. When my mother acquired her first job, she knew no one in L.A., and had no references. Today a job applicant is expected to dress well. Today poor children feel entrenched in poverty and simply having a parent who is imaginative is not enough. And who has any imagination left when one's spirit is ground into the earth by a lack of food and proper shelter?

In my work as an analyst, many clients have expressed the fear that one day they will become a bagperson, pushing a cart around the streets of L.A. Beneath their veneer of success, there is an inner figure of a homeless wretch. We know that in the poor individual there exists an inner figure that may be rich, possessing everything beyond imagination. The rich and the poor are shadows of one another. Jung wrote that the most necessary work in our lifetime is the reconciliation of the opposites within ourselves. In addition, I believe it is time to reconcile the opposites within society. It is past time that the poor can count on medical insurance, a roof over their head, food in their belly, and the possibility of a job.

During the 1980s when interest rates at a savings and loan were 25% and the rich were getting richer, Reagan's idea of helping the unfortunate in our society was called "trickle-down" economics. Somehow the wealth of the corporations at the top would trickle down to the poor. Well, it did not. Reagan also believed that people should pull themselves up by their own bootstraps. Apparently, he never once considered what people would do if they did not have boots at all.

Being poor causes feelings of shame in children. Being different feels shameful to a child. Wearing clothes that are different creates shame in a child. Even eating food that is different from what their friends eat can have that effect. Children who grew up during the Depression are marked in adulthood by residues of that shame. And fear. Deep down there is fear, like a quiet hum, that never quite goes away. One learns to live with it.

Chapter 3

BIRTH'S CRUEL SECRET

"I Am My Own Lost Mother to My Own Sad Child"

Originally published in
Chiron: A Review of Jungian Analysis[5]

The most difficult aspect in writing this paper came with the recollection of my own abandonment as an infant. I was abandoned by my father. In the loss of that relationship, the maternal archetype also was damaged and not able to be carried by my mother. This early abandonment has shaped my life and has colored almost everything I have done in terms of creativity, ambition, and a desire to find ways to nurture myself. Children like me possess an early awareness, a knowing that they are born into a more difficult situation, and this may make them more cautious and watchful. These qualities can be an enormous help in later life if they do not cause isolation.

The Great Goddess came into my life through active imagination and dreams in analysis. She watched over me and helped nourish me. My relationship with the positive mother archetype clearly came about through my contact with a woman analyst. But the relationship to the "good father" came with my marriage, and the nurturing masculine was as much the "lost mother" as was the feminine. I hope it is understood that in speaking of this "lost mother," I am speaking of that which nur-

---

5 Gilda Frantz. "O, I Am My Own Lost Mother to My Own Sad Child," *Chiron: A Review of Jungian Analysis* (1985): 157-172. Reprinted with permission of Chiron Publications.

tures us spiritually. I submit the following material with deep gratitude for all that the gods have given to me, both good and bad.

I chose the title from a scrap of paper I found in my late husband's desk. Its cryptic meaning was numinous and touched me in the place of my own experience of abandonment: it seemed a poetic image of the suffering child.

"*Child* means something evolving toward independence. This it cannot do without detaching itself from its origins: abandonment is therefore a necessary condition, not just a concomitant symptom."[6] There are some for whom the necessary condition of abandonment comes before they can integrate its purpose or meaning. There are those whose experience begins *in utero*, children whose mothers are ill or depressed or die in childbirth or have been abandoned or whose birth is unwanted. There are those mothers who are unwed and offer the child for adoption with great suffering and reluctance. The result of these fateful births is that the lives of child and parents are deeply affected.[7] This is akin to being born into the archetype of the abandoned one; this child has the fate of having to integrate the inner nurturing mother, as well as the inner abandoned child at some point in his or her life. Orphans are particularly prone to this path as are children of narcissistically wounded mothers.[8] What about the child who did not suffer any of the above circumstances?

This child's abandonment comes through the lack of special nurturing by a mother who is not capable of such. The child can feel abandoned even though the outer circumstances of his or her life imply the opposite. Fate intensifies the already intense relationship between parent and child. While the fate of a child is restricted to the parents, the fate of an adult is not limited to the parents.[9] I will say more about this in the case material about Anne, which follows.

---

6 C.G. Jung, "The Psychology of the Child Archetype," CW 9i, ¶ 287.
7 Marion Woodman, "Psyche/Soma Awareness," (paper presented at Conference of Jungian Analysts in New York, May 3–6, 1984).
8 Nathan Schwartz-Salant, *Narcissism and Character Transformation.*
9 C.G. Jung, "The Theory of Psychoanalysis," CW 4, ¶ 343.

Fate and Abandonment

We make certain decisions in life and can avoid this or that, or decide when to marry and whom, but even those decisions send us in a direction that can seal our fate. "Humanity may possibly draw the conclusion that only one side of fate can be mastered with rational intentions."[10] But again, the use of the rational will is only one-half of the picture. The other half is a hurtling toward a destination which we did not choose and which we cannot change. The Stoics called that "the compulsion of the stars," or *Heimarmene.*

A common thread I observe in the people I see analytically is fate. Some have difficult lives, and not all the difficulty is earned. It is not always something they have or have not done that causes them to be abandoned. Often it is the so-called accident of birth that determines their fate. The challenge is to see what each one of us can do with the raw material of life. Life itself is an experiment and, as Emerson puts it, the more experiments we make, the better.

Abandonment is a fateful experience in which we feel we have no choice. We feel alone, as if the gods are not present. If we feel the gods are present and supportive, then we are not abandoned. The word *abandonment* means literally "not to be called." It is etymologically connected with the word *fate*, which means "the divine word" and is from *fari* and *fatum*, meaning "to speak."[11]

Who is it that either summons us or does not? Let us discuss the Fates. They were divine beings who determined the course of human lives and were called Moerae (Moira) by the Greeks and Fata by the Romans, as well as Parcae. The Fates were the daughters of Nyx; their names were Klotho, Lachesis, and Atropos. Klotho means the one who weaves the thread; Lachesis, the one who spins the thread; and Atropos, the one who is unyielding and cuts the thread. Homer repeatedly referred to these three in writing about the destinies allotted to man by the gods. The sisters were always represented as spinning, measuring, and cutting the thread of life. The word shroud is from the root "to

---

10   C.G. Jung, "The Problem with Attitude Type," CW 7, ¶ 73.

11   Joseph T. Shipley, *Dictionary of Word Origins.*

cut." Though there are many contradictions as to whether the Fates did the gods' will, it is evident that even Zeus was bound by their decisions.

The Fates and the Erinyes have a connection. The Erinyes were called the Furies by the Romans and were born from earth fertilized by drops of blood from the castrated Uranus. Aeschylus described them as hideous and frightening, but in sculpture and paintings they are not thus depicted. In their deeds the Erinyes were not regarded as unjust or even malign, even though they were said to inflict punishment. The retribution they meted out was considered a protection of those that human law had failed to protect, such as those who were injured by members of their own families.

The three Graces are associated with the Erinyes and the Fates as well. They were the Eumenides, the kindly ones. The combination of terrible and benign is frequently found in chthonic deities. Spirits, demons, deities, as well as heroes, were thought to live in or beneath the earth, and their concern was with the dead or with the fertility of the earth. Many of the chthonic divinities combined these two functions of punishing and kindness, fertilization and death. Those spirits who lived in the earth where the dead were buried and crops arose inevitably came to be associated with both events.

During the process of thinking about abandonment, I had a dream. The word used for fate in my dream was *bashert*, a Yiddish word meaning "that which is meant is meant." As Dr. Clara Zilberstein interprets it, *bashert* means that something has to happen at a certain moment in time. It is a semi-mystical concept that has to do with who has been promised to a person, one's intended. There is a genuine affection for the word among Jewish people, and it implies a true acceptance of what God gives us, good or bad. For me it implied that the unconscious accepted the presentation of this material—that it was "meant"—and that it focused me upon my fate as a Jewish woman, wife, and widow as well as on my having to deal with "what was intended by the fates."

"Without necessity nothing budges, the human personality least of all. It is tremendously conservative, not to say torpid. Only acute necessity is able to rouse it."[12] Suffering and abandonment awaken us.

---

12 C.G. Jung, "The Development of Personality," CW 17, ¶ 293.

Through the awesome pain of not being called, we may find a way to change what needs changing in our lives. Alchemy says it this way:

> One of the beginning stages of the alchemical work is very often *liquefactio*, the turning into liquid in order to undo the *prima materia*, which is often hardened or solidified in a wrong way and therefore cannot be used to make the philosopher's stone. The minerals must first be liquified. Naturally, the underlying chemical image is the extraction of a metal from its ore through melting, but *liquefactio* often has the alchemical connotation of a dissolution of the personality in tears and despair.[13]

A flame applied externally to melt the metals is alternately raised and lowered in intensity. The raising and lowering of the flame is the agony of abandonment. The flame is Fate.

Tears and Abandonment

In the practice of analytical psychology, it is a common experience to have a patient enter analysis in the stage where there is death and mourning. The condensation of these vapors comes in the form of tears.

Kieffer Frantz[14] did a survey of the literature, which included the then-current psychoanalytic position. He wrote the following:

> These characteristics would seem to be the most consistent observable evidence of the presence of depression. Yet, if we are not to accept a pathological evaluation as being the only point of view, how are we to appraise the observable phenomenon of depression?
>
> Let us begin with the dream of a woman who began therapy in a depression. The dream was that the dreamer was crying and tears were rolling down her cheeks. As the tears were rolling, they gradually turned into diamonds. The tears would certainly seem to substantiate the characteristics of hopelessness, helplessness, sadness and internal suffering described

---

13   Marie-Louise von Franz, *Creation Myths.* 1972/1995, 196.
14   Kieffer Frantz in an unpublished paper on depression from 1966.

above. But what of the diamonds? A definite change has occurred. In *Two Essays on Analytical Psychology* Jung states, "This transformation is the aim of the analysis of the unconscious. If there is no transformation it means that the determining influence of the unconscious is unabated and that it will, in some cases, persist in maintaining neurotic symptoms in spite of all our analysis and all our understanding. Alternatively, a compulsive transference will take hold, which is just as bad as a neurosis."[15]

The dream points to a process that begins with tears and changes or is transformed to diamonds, the "pure water." The depression from this point of view may be conceived as the descent into the unconscious for the purpose of beginning the journey. Between the beginning and the ending there are many different stages and perhaps many depressions.

My interest in tears as a *creative* expression of abandonment began with my reading of the paper, when an acquaintance asked me to find the aforementioned reference to tears and diamonds. The tears are the expression par excellence of abandonment. But what about the diamonds?

Diamond means "invincible." It is also called "adamantine," and from this we get our word "adamant." While adamant means "a very hard substance," it also means "to tame," "to conquer."[16] Metaphorically, nature has to suffer in order to produce a diamond because of the enormous pressure and heat the earth has to sustain to turn carbon into diamonds. In the dream, diamonds evolve from tears. Through the operation of *liquefactio*, the washing away of an encrusted and improperly hardened *prima materia*, jewels are revealed. Thus, the dreamer is given some hope that something valuable may result from her intense suffering.

The diamond body is the Self that is within each of us.[17] Consciousness of the Self shapes and polishes this diamond, and upon our physical death the body drops away and this diamond is revealed in all its dazzling beauty. In von Franz's words:

15 C.G. Jung, "Two Essays on Analytical Psychology," CW 7, ¶ 342.
16 William W. Skeat, *Etymological Dictionary of the English Language*.
17 John Blofeld, *Bodhisattva of Compassion: The Mystical Tradition of Kuan Yin*.

Already in this lifetime you use your diamond body more and more as a dwelling place, so that at the moment of death, like a skin which falls off a fruit, this mortal body falls away and the glorified body—or in Eastern language, the diamond body—is already there. The glorified body, a sort of immortal substance as carrier of the individual personality, is already produced by religious practice during one's lifetime.[18]

In the example used, the diamond is revealed through the process of depression, or *nigredo*, and "conscious suffering."

In writing about her long relationship with Jung, Hilde Kirsch says: "The most important gift Jung has given me, and hopefully to mankind, is the acceptance of suffering as a necessity." In her paper, she quoted a letter he wrote to a friend about suffering: "Try to apply seriously what I have told you, not that you might escape suffering—nobody can escape it—but that you may avoid the worst—blind suffering." Jung also wrote about himself:

I think that God in turn has bestowed life on me and has saved me from petrification. Thus I suffered and was miserable, but it seems that life was never wanting and even in the blackest night . . . by the grace of God I could see a great light. Somewhere there seems to be a great kindness in the abysmal darkness of the Deity.[19]

The dreamer above had the experience of conscious suffering, not of blind suffering. She was aware of her suffering and possibly knew the cause. I was once told by a victim of a disaster that "without this I would have been an ordinary housewife, but this loss forced me to change and now I have developed into a deeper person."

The symbolism of tears and abandonment is found in myths where creation is formed out of tears or by crying. Creation is also brought about by the loneliness of the gods. There is a Baluba myth in which the tears of the animals soften the earth and provide a place for the seeds

18   von Franz, *Creation Myths*, 1972/1995, 331.
19   Hilde Kirsch, "Reveries on Jung," (paper presented at the annual conference of Society of Jungian Analysts of Northern and Southern California, 1975).

to grow and become shelter for the animals.[20] In the Grimm's fairy tale "The Handless Maiden," the daughter is sold to the devil and is saved by her tears. When the devil asks to buy everything behind the mill, the father, unaware that his only daughter is there, sells the property to him. This abandonment of the daughter and subsequent betrayal is what provoked the tears that ultimately save her.

Cinderella is also abandoned by her father. After the death of her mother, the father remarries and she becomes part of what today would be known as a "blended family." Her stepsisters are treated as more important than Cinderella. When the father asks the sisters what they want from town, they ask for precious and costly gifts. As an afterthought, he asks Cinderella, and she only desires a branch from a tree that brushes his hat as he rides home. He forgets all about her after buying the stepdaughters their gifts, but his hat does brush the branch, causing him to remember. Cinderella plants the branch and a tree grows up. A bird comes to the tree and grants Cinderella three wishes. This bird is the spirit of her dead (lost) mother. The story of Cinderella is a beautiful example of the sad child redeeming the lost mother and the abandoning father through her relationship to the Prince.

"What has been spoiled by the mother can only be healed by the mother, and what has been spoiled by the father can only be healed by the father."[21] Relationship itself can often be the healing "father" and can heal a wounded child and be a nurturing parent. We think we find a father in a man, but he may also be a good mother. In the *Bodhisattva of Compassion*,[22] Kuan Yin was masculine and remained so until the twelfth century, when He became a goddess and feminine. The masculine offers its own kind of nurturing.[23]

"The one who hears the cries" is how Kuan Yin is known. This myth is an ancient affirmation of the existence of abandonment and suffering and healing. In Tibetan Buddhism there is the concept of *dukkha*, which, loosely translated, means "suffering," but which can also mean

---

20   von Franz, *Creation Myths.*

21   *I Ching*

22   John Blofeld, *Bodhisattva of Compassion.*

23   Glenn Foy, "On Feeling: The Feeling Function Revisited." (paper presented at the 13th Biennial Bruno Klopfer Workshop, Asilomar, CA, 1983).

"unsatisfactoriness." Suffering, in the Buddhist tradition, is understood to be "within one's 'own' mind and body and when it is understood one will know true happiness." *Dukkha* may be physical pain or mental anguish; it refers to the facts of "birth, old age, disease and death" and to human conditions common to all, such as "grief, lamentation (crying out), pain, anguish and despair."[24]

Weeping often accompanies the sowing of corn. It is the weeping and bewailing the death of the fertility god that ensures his return in the spring.[25] When we cry out in despair, we cry tears and hope that someone hears our cries. Water is the living power of the psyche. When weeping and water symbolism occur during analysis, it calls for a sense of containment and at the same time is a purifying experience.

Lily was in her 50s when she came to see me. Her adult life had been spent having babies, and she had a family of 12 sons and daughters. She found time only for her husband's and children's needs. She felt she had betrayed something within herself in sacrificing her inner child by mothering all those children. Everything made her cry—happiness, sadness, anger, frustration. There were times when it seemed she used an entire box of tissues within an hour. The tears robbed her of a chance to express her feelings; instead of talking, she wept. Her sad child had emerged.

Lily was an abandoned child in that her mother was so self-involved that she was unaware of her daughter's true nature. I sat with Lily through many, many hours of crying, as container for her tears. One day I asked her a question: "Where do all these tears go?" She looked up in amazement and began to describe a deep and vast natural pool or lake that had become filled by her tears. She began a dialogue with her tears, and these dialogues brought old and buried memories up from the depths. Often she recalled wrongs done to her (usually of omission) by parental figures or siblings. She wrote: "I hear the water running down the stream. I locate its site and watch the flow of water. Its movement is suddenly obstructed by an unforeseen obstacle . . . of several rocks falling, disturbing its current and redirecting it toward a new challenge."

---

24   Dalai Lama, the XIVth, *The Opening of the Wisdom Eye*, 142–143.
25   Ad de Vries, *Dictionary of Symbols and Imagery.*

These dialogues between Lily's ego and the unconscious, depicted as her tears, were truly healing. I am not reproducing the entire dialogue out of respect for the organic and ongoing quality of the relationship, but it was active imagination, as opposed to unconscious fantasy. Contact with the unconscious through written dialogue, to use one example of the ways to make the connection, occurs when the ego makes way for the unconscious by lowering its hold (voluntarily), thus allowing archetypal energies a voice.[26] This is how Lily was able to come to a deeper relationship to her tears, by encountering them within herself.

Lily's sad child was a child of the "earth and of starry heaven" and was parched and dry and needed the water of memory. She needed to remember, to take what had been dismembered and lost. By drinking her fill of the cold water of Osiris[27] she could speak to the inner lost mother of her sadness and mourning.

Abandonment and the Creative Child

Etymologically, the word *mourning* means "to remember" and stems from the same root as *memory*. In mourning we are held in the memory of what has been lost or abandoned until we have found a replacement for it. Mourning occurs whether we have ever experienced actual death or not. Most of us enter analysis in a state of deep grief and mourning. Mourning and depression are the other names of abandonment.

Anne came into analysis when *I* was still feeling abandoned and in mourning over the loss of my husband. It was a synchronistic moment. Being in that state myself I could see that she, too, was mourning a loss. Her presenting complaint had to do with many fears about so-called little things. She was reclusive and inclined not to answer her phone. As her story came out, it became apparent that some years before she had suffered the loss of a cherished goal. Perhaps what was lost was the illusion of this possibility in her life.

She had studied to be an actress from the age of seven or eight. At a crucial point in her studies, when she was around twenty, she felt she

---

26 Janet Dallet, "Active Imagination in Practice," in *Jungian Analysis,* 173-191.
27 Jane Ellen Harrison, *Prolegomena to the Study of Greek Religion.*

just didn't have what it took to be an actress, and she didn't feel tough enough. She had planned to study in New York with a famous acting coach, and with almost no reflection, she swiftly gave up her dream. This termination of her career deeply wounded the inner child.

Anne's mother was a strong, opinionated woman, and Anne was under the influence of a powerful negative mother archetype. She was used to having others determine her destiny, but she didn't count on what the loss of her dream would mean to her. In the 1970s she became interested in drugs and found some comfort in them, but this was no solution. Although she was now out of college and had another career in teaching, she often contemplated suicide because of the lack of meaning in her life. She was, in a spiritual sense, half alive. She didn't know she was grieving for her lost ambition, her abandoned career; she only knew she thought about death a great deal. The neurotic perpetually hesitates entering into life and is inclined to avoid the "dangerous struggle for existence." "Refusing to really experience life forces him/her to deny life and thus they 'commit partial suicide'."[28]

My own loss experience had changed me. When I went back to work after my husband's death, I found that a gauzy veil that had formerly existed had disappeared. The veil could be called a "professional attitude." Through my bereavement, an almost ego-less state, my psyche was more permeable, more open to the unconscious. I was less defended and more "there." It was almost as though there were trails of smoke, like those from a Bushman's fire, that circled between Anne and me. I became conscious of the presence of the healing power of the mother for the inner child.

Anne's dreams were frightening to her, yet they showed me that she had the ego strength for the journey and that the journey would take time. Gradually she began to consider the idea that the acting she loved and had given up so many years ago might be in her life in another form. The idea to work in amateur theater was repugnant, but she did like studying, so she enrolled in some classes with local teachers and began to enjoy the contact with the world of acting. Instead of feeling

---

28 C.G. Jung, "The Song of the Moth," CW 5, ¶ 165.

helpless and identified with the sad child, she was beginning to find the lost mother. She was beginning to nurture herself.

Rather than being related to her inner sad child's needs, Anne had been *identified* with the child. Her destiny was tied to her parents. She feared what would happen to her if they died. She feared abandonment. If she could accept her abandoned goal, she might begin a new relationship to the Self. Recently, she has begun to grow up and enter the adult world, a world she had always identified with death and dying and abandonment. It is not to say that now she is without fears, or that her life is "perfect," but she is more in it and more alive to possibilities yet unknown to her.

Abandonment and Loss

One instance of the "sad child–lost mother" abandonment is widowhood. Occasionally, we wounded children find in a mate the mother and/or father we have been deprived of in our early years. With the death of the spouse, we are plunged once again into the deepest mourning. Then the "child" is out, bewildered and in great pain. It is as though one connects with the mourning of Demeter and Persephone, or of Christ on the cross, asking why God has forsaken him.

Let me encapsulate widowhood so that something about the problem the widow faces in relation to the sad child can be understood.

> The position of widows in many cultures is one of the saddest in society. The simple fact that they were born women ensured their fate. The moment their husbands died, their own function in life was regarded as ended. Often they were destroyed to accompany and serve their dead spouses in the new life beyond death, as they had in his earthly life.[29]

While we are too civilized today to allow widows to be put into the grave, the fact remains that many women live their lives through their husbands. Sylvia was a newly widowed woman. Her husband died quite unexpectedly and suddenly. She was a well-paid journalist, in a profes-

---

29 Lou Taylor, *Mourning Dress: A Costume and Social History*, 48.

sion she enjoyed. She was left with two children, her grief, and her anger. "How dare he do this to me?" she raged. What he "did" soon became clear. Her wounded, shy inner child had found a home within the breast of her husband. He was outgoing and aggressive. She was able to meet the outer world through his protection, and now she was abandoned.

When he died, she no longer felt able to meet the world and that part of her went into the grave. Her task, like Persephone's, would be to bring it back into consciousness or find another outgoing and aggressive partner. If she did not find such a replacement, then what was being lived unconsciously through him would have to be made conscious. This step requires an enormous change in attitude and consciousness and a new vessel for the sad child. The change is difficult: it is not desired; and it is not what one seeks willingly.

The experience of widowhood reconstitutes the abandoned child archetype. The feelings around the death of a significant other, especially a spouse, often are guilt, shame, anger, abandonment, depression, lack of libido, and hope. I think the *shame* and *guilt* directly connect to the tradition of widow murder, wherein the one closest to the deceased went with him or her into the land of the dead. By being alive, we feel guilty and ashamed that for us life goes on. This wilderness experience is one we all have, but the widowed need all the encouragement possible to leave the land of the dead and return to life. The pull away from life is very strong at such times.

In modern life one has the automobile, where one who feels abandoned may contemplate death or find a place to cry alone. The car is now the place of sanctuary, and as such it is the place that can allow for thoughts of death and dying. Not that this implies that the car is used to bring about death, but it is there that death is contemplated. Ask any newly widowed person if he or she uses the car as a place to rage and cry and think of death, and the answer will be affirmative.

Another issue common to widows and widowers has to do with money. Many newly widowed women and men obsess about money. Anxiety about money becomes a substitute for the fear of being on one's own. I have known wealthy individuals who become terrified that they are being cheated or robbed by the lawyers and accountants around them. This also applies to individuals without a great deal of money. They, too, find themselves obsessing about money when, in fact, they are grieving about their loss. While there *are* concerns, there is a special kind of concern the newly widowed express, and I think it is due to the feelings of abandonment and the "child." The newly bereaved feel so helpless and naked, so overwhelmed with the feelings of love, hate, loss, etc., that money anxiety becomes the container for all of the above.

Widow murder was a natural consequence of the belief that the wife's life ended with the death of the spouse. And they were often killed with prescribed ritual. . . . As late as 1857 there was a law in Oyo, in Western Nigeria, ensuring that certain individuals in the king's retinue, including his official mother, various priestesses, as well as the king's favorite wife, all died when he died and by their own hand.[30]

Today, widow murder is practiced in a much subtler form. We don't kill the widow: she is abandoned and becomes invisible. The more a woman is identified with her husband, the more prone she is to feelings of abandonment and desertion. In my own experience, I had a "life of my own," but the body blow of grief that I was experiencing was that my marriage had been a safe container for my inner sad child. Alone I avoided this child, but with my husband it was safe to bring her out from time to time. I hated the idea that I would have to face her alone. But it was either that, or like one of the widows in the Melanesian New Hebrides, where a conical cap made of spider's web was used for smothering them, I would be smothered by being stuck in isolation and abandonment.

> When widows were permitted to stay alive, the problem of what to do with them had to be resolved by her own or her husband's relatives. Often she was regarded with suspicion and suspected of witchcraft, because of her contact with death, and the. . . fear that she might have caused her husband's death. In societies where a widow was allowed to remain alive she had to be ritually freed from contact with her dead partner before anyone could touch her or go near her, as death was believed to be very contagious. After a period

---

30 Taylor, *Mourning Dress*, 49.

of isolation she was permitted to re-enter her family in the unenviable new widow's role. The isolation of the widow continues to this day even in the Western world.[31]

In Victorian times the term "widow's weeds" were used to describe the clothing the widows wore. This expression can be traced etymologically to the word *wadmal*, which is a strong, woven cloth. The word encompasses two meanings: *wad*, meaning "a tied bundle," and *mal*, meaning "time." Widow's weeds can imply a limit of time for the mourning period or the isolation, but to me the connotation of strong cloth indicates that the garment is made to last a lifetime.

It is not widely known outside of religious life that Catholic nuns took their habit from the garb widows wore. Sister Mary Patricia Sexton told me that, in and around the seventeenth century in France, nuns could go to rough waterfront dives to do the work of the Church knowing that no one would look at them or bother them if they dressed like widows. The symbolism of marriage to Christ in mourning clothes has other meanings but from the standpoint of this paper, it is interesting to muse about what it was the widows and nuns had in common. Many early convents were started by widows. The clothes they wore were designed to be unchanging and to disguise their sexuality. This outfit, this attitude, was meant to last forever.[32]

In certain tribes a ban was imposed on remarriage until the body of the dead husband had decomposed. The New Zealand Maori widow wore two special feather cloaks called "cloak of tears." The bones were eventually exhumed, wrapped in the feather cloaks, and reburied. Then the widow was free to remarry.[33]

In contemporary times words about death may be included in marriage vows. Yet, of all the widows and widowers I have asked, only one recalls actually hearing the words, "till death do us part" at the wedding. "Attempts to expel death or not to take death into account are a deception committed by man upon himself. No matter how hard man tries to

---

31 Taylor, *Mourning Dress*, 51.
32 Taylor, *Mourning Dress*, 48-56.
33 Taylor, *Mourning Dress*, 56.

shelve and hush up knowledge of the inevitable end of his earthly life, he never quite succeeds."[34]

Conclusion

Analytical psychology encourages individuals to give up attitudes that are too conventional or too collective and stifling. From the history of widow murder, it can be seen that within each of us there is a powerful, archaic pull to abandonment. I encourage analysands who are grieving to be "different," that is, to be true to what the soul wants. A relationship to the fantasies and inner world is an appropriate counterbalance to the forces of the collective consciousness that are inclined to isolate the abandoned one and are often destructive to his or her development. There is a journey to the underworld which the sad child makes. He or she becomes intimate with the dark, with fear, and with what can be the most decisive experience, that of being alone with our own self. Before we experience this, something we treasure is sacrificed and/or lost, abandoned. We have to become disidentified from the oneness of subject and object, from unconsciousness *participation mystique.*

To feel abandoned is to be in a state of constant connectedness to the lost object.[35] There is a time in the mourning process when there is a serenity in the bereaved, a time of grace. The journey to the underworld is a rite of passage and must be seen as such. One must cross the river and return again, alone. The danger is getting stuck halfway between one shore and the other. How many of us still mourn a childhood which was not what we wished for?

Next to the well of Mnemosyne stands the forbidden well of Lethe, forgetfulness. The notion of forgetfulness is that in death we can forget the sorrows of this world and forget the difficult journey to the next. This theme is elemental and human, and it belongs not just to the Greek and Orphic myths but occurs everywhere.[36]

---

34 Herman Feifel, *The Meaning of Death*, 124.
35 Gilda Frantz, "Are We All Widows?" (paper presented at Knowing Woman Conference, Los Angeles, 1980).
36 Jane Ellen Harrison, *Prolegomena to the Study of Greek Religion.*

Forgetfulness can be an obstacle on this journey. When childhood dreams or fantasies are recalled in the process of analysis, healing can occur. These memories have been hidden away to protect them. But if they are hidden forever, one can remain stuck in the sadness and mourning. A woman recalls a secret game played in childhood. She was an alchemist and invented the perfect food that would stamp out hunger in the world. This game was an attempt on the part of her unconsciousness to compensate for not getting the right food from her parents. I think that secret games from childhood are an attempt on the part of the psyche to protect what is healing and precious from the too close scrutiny of the negative parental image. This is also why children often stop drawing or coloring at an early age if the work is criticized by an authority figure. This protects further damage to the expression of the imaginative child's psyche until adulthood when, it is hoped, he or she can begin to allow it out once more.[37]

The archetypes of the sad child and the lost mother emerge during times of intense loss and suffering and abandonment. Jung himself had such an experience after his break with Freud. A memory came to him with intense affect about himself as a young boy of 10 or 11. He remembered that as a child he liked to play with sand and stones and make castles and such. He realized that he had forgotten this young lad, but it was obvious to Jung that the child was still alive and wanted something from him. Jung proceeded to do whatever the inner child wished, carefully noting the images and fantasies that were activated by the contact. He called this activity "serious play." This occurred during the time that Jung was in despair over the loss of his relationship to Freud, as well as over his professional direction and life course.

Through this serious play, Jung made contact with his forgotten and abandoned child and brought the child into his life. You might say that he became the lost mother to his own sad child. Through contact with this inner child came a burst of creativity. In the film *Matter of Heart*,[38] von Franz said that whenever Jung was about to begin writing a book, he would go to the shore of the lake and dig in the sand and make

---

37   Gilda Frantz, "Images and Imagination: Wounding and Healing," (paper presented at the C.G. Jung Institute of San Francisco, 1980.)

38   *Matter of Heart,* 1986.

passages for the water to flow. He did not allow that inner child to be forgotten again.

What happens to many of us is that we allow the child to emerge within the vessel of relationship and often seek a relationship in which the child can come out into the open and play. When this container is broken by death or divorce or some separation of an abandoning nature, the child goes into hiding and suffers. Many have had this experience of bringing an abandoned, sad child into a relationship so that the other could nurture the child. When this occurs, the union can become a sacred vessel for the inner creative child or a substitute for a relationship to this child.

Chapter 4

ON THE MEANING OF LONELINESS

Originally presented at the *Chaos to Eros Conference*[39]

I'm glad Dr. Wesley told the audience that I am a widow because Mr. Gene Adams, a researcher and friend of mine, told me about an article in the *International Journal of Psychoanalysis* called "A little widow is a dangerous thing!" Consider yourselves warned.

Do any of you know why I am the second person speaking today? I think it's because when we were planning the conference, one of the men said that he thought it was a good idea to have a woman after lunch. I suppose the subject of loneliness is better taken in with a full stomach rather than an empty one.

Before I begin this talk, I want to say that although I am going to dwell on loneliness and aloneness as psychic states of being, I want you all to know that I realize that it isn't easy to be alone in these times of "sharing" and "instant intimacy." About the only room left in most homes which is absolutely private, is the bathroom. And it is hard, especially for women, to go out socially with dignity if one is alone. What can be done about that, I don't know, but I felt I should say that I know there are problems in the outer world with being alone even if one choses to be by oneself, and likes it. Rooms in hotels are more expensive. Singles and unmarried people are burdened by higher taxes. But all that aside, perhaps this conference will help us find that being alone can be a rewarding experience.

---

39 Gilda Frantz, "On the Meaning of Loneliness," (paper presented at the *Chaos to Eros Conference*, Los Angeles, October, 1976).

Divorcee. Widow. Widower. Homosexual. Alcoholic. Bachelor. Spinster. Single. These individuals have something in common, namely, that universal, archetypal condition called loneliness. These individuals are uniquely susceptible to its cold, clutching touch. But what about *you*? What does being by yourself or being lonely mean to *you*?

Do you run from it or do you seek it? Do you like to be by yourself or do you loathe it? Are you yearning for a change in your life and yet are afraid? Have you lost your job? Or broken up with your lover? Are you getting a divorce or have you suffered a loss in a relationship? Are you in the winter of your life or the springtime? Are weekends something you look forward to or something you dread? And how do you feel when the day ends and night begins to fall? Some of what I have spoken of are feelings one has when experiencing loneliness or when alone. The way I see it, loneliness is a feeling of being separated from something, cut off, cast out, abandoned, and forgotten.

Aloneness is the opposite. Feeling good when alone is to feel a sense of contentment and a feeling of connectedness to yourself, of purpose, containment and wholeness. Being alone could be compared to Eros and loneliness to Chaos. But before you have one you have to experience the other. Alone and lonely are, to me, different and when I speak of them you will see these differences.

There is an ancient story called the Gilgamesh Epic which is very beautiful. Dr. Rivkah Kluger has worked on this myth from the understanding of analytical psychology for over 25 years and,unfortunately, her work is not yet available in English.

The myth concerns the development of King Gilgamesh and central to the process he undergoes is his deep love for his friend, Enkidu. Enkidu, a primitive man, teaches him about love and ultimately due to his death, also teaches Gilgamesh about loneliness, and grief. I recommend this book to all of you. But I mention it now because this myth was recorded 2,000 years before the coming of Christ. So you see, the problem of grief and separation and ego/self development has been around since humankind began. And possibly before that. In Genesis 1:3 it says:

> And the earth was without form, and void:
> and darkness was won the face of the waters.
> And God said, Let there be Light: and there was Light.

In the *Gospel According to Thomas*, a Coptic text, Jesus says:

> If he is the same, he will be filled with light,
> but if he is divided, he will be filled with darkness.

What is loneliness? Marie-Louise von Franz sees that it is connected with creation. In her book, *Creation Myths*, she finds that loneliness is one of the reasons given in myths for why God created the world. One myth from an Inca tribe says that God created heaven and earth because he felt lonely. And in the Upanishads Atman "feared and therefore anyone who is lonely fears."[40] So being lonely and afraid is not confined to the human realm.

From the very beginning of time and now we see perhaps before the beginning, loneliness and creation came together and belong together. Von Franz says that in all religions isolation is one of the known techniques by which to meet the gods, or by which we become initiated into an inner experience.

The fear of loneliness is the fear of the unknown—whether within oneself or without. For the purpose of this paper I am going to concentrate on inner states of loneliness, those not necessarily caused by outer events or circumstances. But whether caused by outer loss or inner, the feelings are the same. They are almost identical.

To be lonely is to become aware of one's self; that is—to be aware of the state of being cut off, and separated from something, from the Self. If we do not understand what it is that makes us feel this way, what it means, then that feeling of loneliness returns repeatedly, and we are apt to go through life as sad, lonely people, and often not quite sure why.

Consciousness of Self can be the result of understanding and really experiencing one's loneliness. The big questions, who we are, what we are doing with our lives, whether we are cut off from our inner life or

---

40　R.E. Van Voorst, *The Anthology of World Scriptures*, 30.

perhaps in some cases the outer one, all these aspects of ourselves *can* be more clearly understood, and *need* to be understood.

Loneliness is like waiting for something or someone to enter our lives, but being afraid to open a door and let it in. When we delude ourselves, we think we know what it is we can *do* to disperse the chaos, the loneliness, and often we find that those efforts only heighten the loneliness rather than dispel it.

There is a plum tree in my garden that bears fruit. When it was a slender sapling, a potted plant was hung from one of its limbs and we forgot about it. When we realized what we had done, it was too late, for the wire from which the pot was suspended had grown into the limb and was imbedded forever. The bark had become very thick around the wounded place. The tree continued to grow, the limb continue to grow and even gave fruit with this wire in its flesh. To me, that tree is a symbol of how growth and suffering go together and how our growth continues even though most of us carry a wound of one kind or another.

I think it's important to say that I am not here today at this conference because I am an expert in loneliness (or in being alone). All of us are experts in being lonely, since next to birth and death it is the most universally experienced state of being. And in that order: birth, loneliness, death. Men and women sometimes say that they have never felt the bliss of falling in love, but I have never heard anyone say they have never been lonely. There are degrees of loneliness, of course, some being much deeper and more lasting than others, but they are all related.

Loneliness has to do with development, with the process of individuation, with becoming. Perhaps, together, we can try to see how that can be observed and experienced and how we can go from loneliness to aloneness. Or as Dr. Jung once put it, from chaos to cosmos.

Mother Teresa of Calcutta, who is called "the apostle of the unwanted," says: "The biggest disease today is not leprosy, or tuberculosis, but rather the *feeling* of being unwanted, uncared for and deserted . . . the greatest evil is the lack of love." That feeling of being unwanted and uncared for has to do with loneliness, with being cast out and forgotten. Mother Teresa is the founder of a home for the dying in Calcutta,

India, and yet she speaks of feeling unwanted and lack of love as a worse disease than leprosy![41]

In a recent interview in *Ebony* magazine, Al Greene, a rock singer, said that even in a concert attended by 40,000 people, he often feels lonely. And a friend told me that she deals well with being divorced and alone until she goes out socially. Then she becomes painfully aware of being alone when seeing *couples* everywhere.

What then *is* loneliness? Is it the cancer of the spirit? Is it being without companionship? Many of us know certain individuals who live without companionship and are not lonely, but, rather, lead rich full lives.

In *Courage to Create*, Rollo May says that Sartre, Kierkegaard, and Camus all agree on the meaning of courage, and that courage is involved in this process of being without companionship and not lonely. Courage is described as the capacity to move ahead in spite of despair, not in the absence of despair. Loneliness is a condition in which one feels as though everything ceases to move, where we feel cut off from life, isolated and stuck. It's like the tar baby story when Brer Rabbit gets stuck in the tar and is rescued only by his quick wit and being thrown into the briar patch. Aloneness would be the capacity to move on in spite of despair.

The subject today brought a certain amount of chaos into my life, and I have lived these past weeks with books and papers strewn about my house, hoping that there was some thread that would lead out of the chaos into Eros or relatedness. And I finally did have a dream, which I'll tell you later.

In the midst of that chaos I turned to my dictionary, that splendid treasure house of order and knowledge. To know what a word means, where it came from, is a little like knowing the last name of your daughter's boyfriend. It may not change anything, but it is very reassuring!

The trip through the dictionary brought order into my chaos, and also some understanding of the words I am using today. Take the word *alone*. Alone means: al one. All one. Totally one. And one is defined as:

---

41 Malcolm Muggeridge, as cited in Keefer, *Let's Get Committed: First Lesson Sermons for Sundays After Pentecost*, 14.

undividable. So we might say that if one is alone, that person is an individual, cannot be split, and is totally one.

I also looked up *separate* (sep'e rāt) or separate (sep' rit) and discovered it means: prepare to be apart, which must be the reason that people who are having trouble in their marriages say: "We've separated." It's a preparation sometimes for divorce, sometimes not.

Separate, single, solo, solitude, solitary, and *suicide* all come from the same root and by implication are related to orphan and widow (which I will talk about a little later).

In *A Year with C.S. Lewis* N.W. Clerk says that often if we want something too badly, it just doesn't happen. An example of this is saying to a friend, "Now we must have a really good talk," and getting silence. Or saying to ourselves that we must get a good night's sleep and ushering in hours of wakefulness. Similarly, he says, "it is the very intensity of longing that draws the iron curtain, that makes us feel that we are staring into a vacuum."[42]

And yet, that condition of wanting something badly has caused countless people to go to singles bars, dances, and clubs hoping for a solution to their intense longing. Advertisements for such places say that if you find the right partner, meet people, etc., your troubles are over. They advise us to turn off from stress, turn off anger, turn off reflection, and turn on to serene and happier living. If we learn to deal with the problems that are unique to singles—namely, coping, communicating, and negotiating with each other—then we will be happy. And they ask: "Are *YOU* in charge of your life?"

The implication is that if the outer realm is okay, then you're okay. The iron curtain is drawn over loneliness, its value is denied. We are deceiving ourselves if we think that by doing all that, the loneliness will get less, for in truth it becomes more powerful. In a straightforward book called *Lonely in America*, by Suzanne Gordon, she speaks about "the loneliness business," referring to places which make money out of loneliness. Gay and singles bars thrive on people who keep coming back again and again and do not become paired in any meaningful way. These enterprises profit from hit-and-miss relationships.

---

42 N.W. Clerk, *A Year with C.S. Lewis*, 301.

I feel that loneliness is valuable and essential for human development and should not be ignored, avoided, or masked. That only makes it worse and more painful. And all of us know that loneliness is painful enough without making it more so. John Perry, author of *The Far Side of Madness*, in speaking about the acute psychotic process, says: "The psyche is already busy with its own aims to repair the situation. In fact, we discern that the psyche has drawn the individual into this predicament for a very good reason, to bring about some very much needed changes in the organization of the Self and the emotional life.[43]" Couldn't the same thing be said about the chaos of loneliness? That we are plunged into this state by the psyche in order to bring about a separation from the old way of perceiving and being? In approaching the unknown, the new, many of us feel dread, fear, and apprehension.

Loneliness is connected to that feeling and is like a wall that surrounds a threshold that we must cross if we are to develop and grow. That is not to say that certain individuals who rush through life "doing" things have the answer, or even that doing things helps. It's a paradox.

If we feel lonely in the midst of a happy marriage, or other relationship, or at a social gathering, or even a conference such as this, that feeling demands that we understand it and interpret what it is and what it is saying. At home alone we tend to feel less isolated than when we are with others . . . as though social contacts remind us of what is painful.

If a child complains to his mother that he has nothing to do and is lonely, the mother might try to help fill that void, maybe, but what the child is saying to her is that he is on the verge of stepping over a threshold, growing up, changing, and he is experiencing that as loneliness, as "nothing to do," the abyss. This condition of loneliness, as it is related to thresholds, goes with us through life, from one development to another, and there is a reason for it.

The repetition of loneliness is similar to taking a train to, say, Santa Fe. The first time you go there you experience it one way. If you go back again, it's still Santa Fe, but now you have more knowledge and possibly will see it differently. That's how loneliness is: You may go there again, but if you really look at it, you will experience it differently each time.

---

43 John Weir Perry, *The Far Side of Madness*, 140.

Although other events such as loss of job or having your children go away from home or giving birth or going through menopause or a death in the family can all produce that sense of loneliness and chaos, it can also happen the same way with no outer stimulus. To feel lonely without "reason" is like being in a state of mourning with no one to mourn except yourself.

We feel lonely when we leave someone or when someone leaves us. I think it makes little difference who does the leaving. Children going off to camp or school for the first time usually feel very lonely the first day or night, and their parents often feel the same way, feeling what they might be feeling. Jung calls this type of intimate relationship a *participation mystique*, and I will say more about that a little later. But for now, I just want to say that it is that connection to another that makes one suffer when a separation occurs. In mythology, that can be seen in myth. When Persephone was taken away into the underworld, Demeter was so lonely for her that she caused the earth to stop blooming. When that bond is broken it feels like death and we suffer until we are reunited with that person (in Demeter's case it was her daughter) or with that within ourselves from which we have become alienated, causing a feeling of separation.

Images of this separation are Odysseus's journey, the story of Job, and, of course, Demeter and Persephone. Another image of separation could be Sleeping Beauty. In that story she and all the people in the castle must sleep until a certain handsome prince finds and kisses Sleeping Beauty. Until love, personified by the prince, came along, all slept and it was like death, and brambles overgrew the walls until the castle was hidden from view. It was hard for love to enter, and many young men tried but had to give up. When love did enter, and it was his kiss which awoke Sleeping Beauty, the enchantment was broken and life began to flow again. There are people like that, who are so walled in that even though they yearn for love, they make it difficult for love to enter, and it can take a long time for someone to find the courage to awaken them from their unconsciousness.

Although in this fairy tale everyone awoke as though nothing had happened, in reality, rebirth, waking up, can be a frightening and painful experience. In some ways it can be more frightening than the abyss. Being asleep demands very little from us; it is cool, numbing and we are totally oblivious. There is no action, no stumbling steps, nothing. But to be reborn is to be plunged first into chaos and then to emerge into an alien place where you don't know if there is hospitality or hostility, or even how to speak this new language. Rebirth, emergence from chaos, is not always a good feeling and does not happen without some powerful experience. Even though people often say, "Wow, death and rebirth," it doesn't come without painful discovery.

Loneliness is the state of becoming, and aloneness is the state of being. The difference between the two is what gives loneliness meaning. It is the problem of those opposites that Jung writes about in most of his books, the problem of the very meaning of life. To be alone and not lonely is to be victorious over chaos; it is the treasure hard to attain and the pearl of great value. To be alone and not lonely is to be in contact with the inner divine; that inner light in which there is no darkness and no fear.

In *Ancient Incubation and Modern Psychotherapy*, C.A. Meier says that loneliness is divinely sent, the wound which makes us nearer to the Self, to God. Gerhard Adler speaks of psychic birth as being experienced as a sense of loneliness.[44] That is, when we are in that process there is often an acute loneliness preceding it.

When we are in this state of psychic birth and we feel lonely, it is necessary that we try to understand what the underlying cause is for the loneliness. Unfortunately, the outer collective says, "No, you shouldn't feel lonely," and tries to help you do something about it. The outer collective attitude is that no one should suffer the feeling of loneliness, even though there are a lot of people who are lonely in this world. Some of the solutions collectively oriented persons try are drinking, changing jobs, meeting someone new, getting a divorce, or taking a cruise. But the idea is to *do* something. Being by oneself in present society is tantamount to admitting one is a failure, and the urge to do something is based upon this feeling. While I am all for love, romance, cruises, dat-

---

44 Gerhard Adler, "Personal Encounters with Jung," in *Dynamics of the Psyche,* 91-93.

ing, etc., I sometimes get angry that there is so little value given to being by oneself . . . at least by some.

In places of dense population such as India and Japan, aloneness is respected. To be *unaccompanied* means, literally, not having someone to eat bread with. No companion. To be by one's self, alone or lonely, means that one eats bread with oneself . . . it can be a rich and often satisfying meal.

Loneliness is often caused by the loss of a relationship to someone, but it can come about through loss of relationship to oneself. Again, I am speaking of inner loss, not actual loss. The tears, the sadness, and that inner voice that won't stop asking for "something," all are a necessary part in helping to make us conscious that something is wrong, that we are resisting a new step in our growth, that we are cut off from our own self, and that we cannot continue to live our lives solely from the standpoint of ego directedness. To feel lonely is very much like being in mourning; there is a deep sense of loss.

A man in his late 30s had such an experience. His wife went away for a period of time and due to this separation, he experienced extreme anxiety caused by the panicky feeling that she might never return and that he would be alone, without her. And he wondered how he could live without her. She had a reason for going. They were having difficulties then, but she did eventually return. Yet the grief and dread the man suffered were as great as if she had died suddenly or had actually left, never to come back. It was this dread that brought him to analysis to try to understand what it was that had produced such fear.

In analytical psychology there is a great deal of value given to nonverbal means of reaching the unconscious contents. Jungians often suggest the use of creative means to understand what is going on in the depths. Jung says in his article "The Transcendent Function" that the hands know how to solve a riddle that the mind has wrestled with in vain.[45] And it was in this way that the man began fingerpainting. One of the fingerpaintings he did was of an onion growing out of the earth. I need to reiterate that this is not art but spontaneous work that literally springs from the depths. To the man the image of the onion seed per-

---

45   C.G. Jung ,"The Transcendent Function," CW 8, ¶ 180.

plexing. The only thing he could relate to the onion was its many skins, which he felt he was in the process of peeling away in himself. But there is another meaning to onion. The word itself is related to *unus*, one. And onions have a unique capacity that other vegetables do not have: They make us cry tears . . . in spite of ourselves. Thus, the onion is a special symbol for the development of feeling and for the state of loneliness. There are many old wives' recipes for avoiding the tears of the onion, most of which have to do with holding the breath. Isn't that what we do when we are lonely—try to avoid breathing, try to avoid the tears?

The onion fingerpainting was just what this man needed: the capacity to cry *and* to experience himself as one, whole, and not connected to his wife in that desperate, clinging way. And the painting implied that the possibility of wholeness grew in his own garden, in his own earth, and would come out of chaos.

In an essay on "Psychology and Literature" dealing with the creative process, Jung calls chaos, *pregnant*.[46] That gives it meaning, doesn't it? For if chaos is pregnant, then loneliness becomes a part of the birth process, part of the process of individuation that will bring forth new life. But because of the frightening aspect of the abyss, it is hard to perceive of a process of birth taking place in chaos. Who doesn't feel fear when looking into that blackness? Besides, what can be born out of chaos? The earth? The heavens? Artists live with chaos all of the time if they amount to anything because they understand and respect that their new direction will emerge from that chaos.

To get into a relationship with one's self can only be accomplished with God's help, meaning, with a spiritual attitude toward one's own suffering. C.G. Jung once said that to suffer blindly is the worst suffering of all. We need to ask ourselves, "What do *you* need that I have not been giving you?" Usually we say, *I* need that, but if we ask ourselves, in our depths—"What do *you* need, what have *you* been denied?"—then a change can occur and loneliness can transform into something more.

Jung says that fantasies of utopia lead to their opposite. When we wish for freedom from loneliness, we get increased loneliness. When we wish for the perfect man or the perfect woman, most often we get the

---

46 C.G. Jung, "Psychology and Literature," CW 15, ¶ 141.

opposite—someone who causes us more difficulty and more heartache. It is, Jung says, like a totalitarian state that promises freedom and then enslaves its subjects. So, wishing for the perfect solution to loneliness is not the way to go. It is also important to remember that loneliness is a station on the journey, not the destination itself.

Loneliness is a preparation, not just a separation. A preparation for what, you might ask? A preparation for finding out if we are related to something *infinite*. In *Memories, Dreams, Reflections* Jung calls that the "telling question of our lives," finding out whether we are related to the infinite: "The more a man lays stress on false possessions and the less sensitivity he has for what is essential, the less satisfying is his life."[47] Being lonely can put us in touch with what is false in our lives and what is unessential.

If there is a meaning to loneliness, it is that it forces us into a deeper awareness of the Self, with our inner spiritual guide and our own depth. When we find the *meaning* of our own loneliness it ceases to be a punishment, a forced isolation from which we yearn to escape or be rescued. When we begin to find the meaning, to ask how this is our own doing, we cease to fall victim to the delusion that "all misfortune lies outside" and all help, too.

Male, female; single, married; young, old—we often feel that if we had a lover, or a job, or perhaps youth, or whatever it is that we complex humans desire, then everything would be all right. Maybe. But what then? What if, by chance, we do get what we wish for, then what? I can still remember, as a young married woman with children and what is known as a good life, I had feelings of loneliness and felt very guilty because of those feelings. Often when things outside us are the most harmonious, we become aware that there is something more that demands our consideration, our energy, and we have to pay attention.

In referring to aloneness, Jung says: "It is the highest and most decisive experience of all, . . . to be alone with [our] own self or whatever else one chooses to call the objectivity of the psyche."[48] But before one can

---

47 C.G. Jung, *Memories, Dreams, Reflections*, 325. Note: *MDR* refers throughout this publication to *Memories, Dreams, Reflections*.

48 C.G. Jung, "Introduction to the Religious and Psychological Problems of Alchemy," CW 12, ¶ 32.

come to that "highest and most decisive experience of all," something must be broken, sacrificed, or lost. One must become disidentified from that curious and close psychological bond that Jung describes as "a partial identity which rests on an *a priori* oneness of subject and object."[49]

One example of that "oneness of subject and object" would be a so-called ideal marriage, or mother and child, or sister and brother. This closeness Jung calls the *participation mystique*, and although it is an essential factor in our early development, it can prevent us from coming to a complete experience of self-realization at a later time in our life when that identification with another keeps us from a deeper understanding of ourselves.

The breaking of the *participation mystique* is often viewed as something destructive, negative. We tend to see the end of certain relationships only as a negative happening, just like we tend to think of forest fires as destructive, when in truth it has been said that they are essential to the growth process of the forest. The end of a *participation mystique* also allows new growth, and although it can be experienced as a failure by the ego, it is essential to growth.

Every relationship carries within it the seeds of its own end. No romance, if fully lived to its conclusion, lasts forever in the same state of rapture, and no friendship stays unchanged, no matter how perfect. George Bernard Shaw thinks that God's great joke on humankind is that we feel as though we own one another when, in fact, we are loaned to one another. That's an interesting point of view.

An orphan is a child whose *participation mystique* has been broken too soon, and he or she suffers from that break. Feeling lonely is similar to feeling like an orphan, in a symbolic way, with the sense of desertion and feeling so alone and unprotected. Looking into the orphan as a symbol turned up some interesting things.

An orphan is a child without a father. It is defined that way in my dictionary. To be fatherless is to be without the protection and guidance of the masculine, of that spiritual force which is necessary for development. Often in life, whether we have a father or not, we can *feel* fatherless (or motherless) if that connection to a guiding principle is absent.

---

49 C.G. Jung, "Definitions," CW 6, ¶ 781.

In alchemy, the orphan is synonymous with the *lapis*, the stone. And the stone is often called the orphan, or The One. The alchemists referred to the stone as "orphan" because it was unique, was never seen anywhere else, and they said that it could be found in the Emperor's crown. I am paraphrasing Jung here. Jung thinks that the term *solitaire*, the name of a certain cut of gem, comes from that early definition of "orphan," since it is alone in its setting.

Jung goes on to say that the "orphan" is often referred to as the "son of the widow" and the "children of the widow" and appears to be of Manichaean origin. Hermes Trismegistus placed the orphan and the widow together, the widow being a symbol for the chaos, the *prima materia*.

There are many synonyms in alchemy for the *prima materia* that allude to its virginal or maternal quality. It is that which exists without man and yet is the "matter of all things." *Prima materia* is that out of which the lapis, the stone, the orphan comes (see *Mysterium Coniunctionis*).[50]

There are many references in the Old Testament and the New Testament to orphans and widows, with one of the most touching in Lamentations 5:3: "We are orphans and fatherless, our mothers are as widows." The text goes on to disclaim the wrongs that befall the people because they feel that God has forgotten them: "Wherefore dost thou forget us forever, and forsake us so long time?" (5:20). Perhaps the references to orphans and widows in the Bible really relate to the *prima materia* and the lapis . . . the chaos and the self.

To be an orphan or a widow is to have experienced loss, separation, and to be bereft. The word *bereft* originally meant to "have one's clothes taken away." That would mean a loss of identity, a breaking of that *participation mystique*, that is what makes us feel bereft. And the capacity to wear a new garment would be the capacity for further development. That would be our individuality.

Most of us like to be around lovers. There is a warmth and an innocence that are contagious. But there is also a contagion around grief-stricken people, and where love brings warmth, loneliness brings a chill

---

50   C.G. Jung, *Mysterium Coniunctionis*, CW 14, ¶ 33.

that tends to push people away. And I think that is how nature intended it, because in times of grief or loneliness we need to attend to our own healing. That is not to say that people should be deserted when in trouble, but there is that which needs total attention, and so it isn't by accident that we avoid such individuals. None of us wants to be reminded of the chill of death that we all must face, sooner or later in our lives.

In her complex book, *Number and Time* (which I hasten to say that I have only perused), von Franz says (and this is a slight digression) that in the Mayan religion there is "a trancendental primal god who hovers over all creation and is known as the Single One."[51] Here is another reference to the solitary or single being connected with the divine. And then she tells us that "although a specific day is alloted to each god, only the powers of the underworld, the founders of chaos and meaninglessness, are given no special day on the calendar and to them belong the five nameless days at the end of the year."[52]

Is it possible that our calendar also has forgotten those powers of chaos and meaninglessness? Can there be a better explanation for the chaotic feelings generated during the last week of our year? It makes you wish that those gods had been given a little more respect.

I told you earlier that I'd had a dream. I would like to tell you that dream and then to close with a story.

The dream is very short: *A voice said that it is out of chaos that everything grows.*

Connecting that dream to this conference, I knew that it referred to the creative aspect of chaos, to the unknown. It also told me that it is all right for me to be here today.

My dream reminded me of a novel by Saul Bellow, called *Henderson the Rain King*. All my friends know that I have been in love with Henderson for a long time, ever since the book was published in 1959.

I've since heard that Saul Bellow dictated this book in a matter of a few weeks and it has that raw, spontaneous quality as though it leaped from his unconscious and was born unpolished but promising.

---

51 Marie-Louise von Franz, *Number and Time*, 144.
52 von Franz, *Number and Time*, 144.

Let me tell you a little about Eugene Henderson. He weighed 16 pounds at birth and grew to be a large man, 6-feet 4-inches tall, with a 22-inch neck. Not a giant certainly, but a powerful man. And he has a very large nose, possibly like the pigs he once raised, or more likely like his large ego that sticks itself into everything. Being a millionaire makes him a very special hero, because being poor is not his problem. And he didn't have to make his fortune in order to win the princess the way heroes do in fairy tales . . . but he *did* try to please his rich and success-ful father—and he failed. The more he tried to do things to please his father, the worse things got as you will see. He is, by the way, 55 years old when we first meet him, and has been in the army and studied the violin and been married twice. He is in a state of collapse due to a voice that speaks within him and says over and over, "I want, I want." He has become destructive to himself and to others around him and feels his temper to be the cause of the sudden death of an old lady after she heard him yell at his wife.

The story begins this way: Henderson speaks: "What made me take this trip to Africa?" he asks.

> When I think of my condition when I bought the ticket all is grief. . . . A disorderly rush begins—my parents, my wives, my girls, my children, my farm, my animals, my habits, my teeth, my face, my soul! I have to cry, no, no, get back, curse you, let me alone! But how can they let me alone? They belong to me. They are mine.[53]

It turns into chaos.

Notice the way he speaks about everything as belonging to him? He has a huge ego. Being a pig farmer is no accident, because Henderson has lived his life exclusively on this lower level. Later in the novel, when he is introduced to the pet lion of an African king, he describes his pig nature as having ill-prepared him for this royal meeting.

Caught by his ego demands, Henderson has been the victim of his inner voice, the one that constantly said, "I want, I want." He was a vic-tim because he didn't understand it, and everything he did to quiet the

---

53 Saul Bellow, *Henderson the Rain King*, 3.

voice had no effect at all. In fact, the more he did, the more it repeated itself and the louder it grew. "I want. I want."

He feels desperate. His old ways won't work any longer. His powerful ego, having done it all alone has no sense of worth or accomplishment, so he decides to get away, to go to Africa, the land of mystery, of darkness, the unconscious. And he goes alone.

Jung once quoted the alchemists as saying that whoever is lonely and isolated from the crowd and cannot join other people will find an inner friend to join and guide him or her.

That is what happens to Henderson. He finds a friend, an African guide, who tells Henderson that he will take him far. Together they go into that alien, unfamiliar, and wondrous place that Henderson describes as:

> . . . a region surrounded like a floor by mountains. It was hot, clear, and arid and after several days we saw no human footprints. Nor were there many plants; for that matter there was not much of anything here; it was all simplified and splendid, and I felt I was entering the past. The real past. The prehuman past. And I believed there was something between the stones and me . . . You could see the clouds being born on the slopes. From the rock came a vapor but it was not like ordinary vapor. . . .[54]

I think of Africa as lush, vegetative, paradise, but in the state in which Henderson arrived, it perfectly described his sense of barrenness or aridity. And the vapor that comes from the rock gives a promise that there is more here, much more.

Central to the novel is the feat of strength which Henderson performs. He lifts the statue of a great goddess and by so doing causes the rain to fall and becomes the Rain King. And he meets the King Dafu and develops a great friendship with him which changes his life. The king is educated and has studied medicine and becomes his real guide. It is this friendship that reminds me very much of Gilgamesh and Enkidu, although they are not at all identical.

---

54 Bellow, *Henderson the Rain King*, 46.

Through his friendship with this African king, Henderson learns about himself and is introduced to his own royal nature. He meets the lion and undergoes the initiation of fear.

But the king, his friend, dies, and Henderson is bereft and isolated. He is told that he is to be the new king, not just the rain king. He remembers that the king once told him that to be king is to accept that one day, if he even once cannot perform the duties that the harem demands, he will be killed. And Henderson wisely decides that he doesn't want that and escapes. That's the story essentially. The wisdom of not staying is the wisdom of not becoming identified with the king but of being able to integrate those qualities.

It is a very funny story, and beneath its surface there is the painful human experience of developing a different relationship to the self. Henderson's inner voice was a real problem for him. One day he is telling the king about his voice. He and the king often had such meaningful discussions. The king asks what is the voice demanding and wonders if it has ever said what it wants. Henderson says, "No, it never names names." And the king says, "But whatever it is, how hungry it must be." Then the king has an insight and realizes that it was that *imprisoned want* that gave Henderson the strength to lift the statue of the goddess.

Henderson wants his spirit "to burst its sleep." He yearns to awaken and find himself and we see what his soul has to go through in order to awaken, how it first plunges into chaos and then becomes connected to Eros and the creative.

If the mother of all is chaos, then the father must be the imagination—that which fertilizes. And what is born out of that union is the orphan, the self.

In *Psychology and Alchemy*, Jung says of the concept of *imaginatio* that it is "probably one of the most important if not *the* most important keys to the understanding of the opus."[55] *Imaginatio* was understood by the alchemists:

> to be the key which opens the door . . . to things greater. . .
> . It is the place and the medium of realization which is nei-

---

55   C.G. Jung, "The Projection of Psychic Content," CW 12, ¶ 396.

ther matter nor spirit but that realm of subtle reality which can only be expressed by the symbol. The symbol is neither abstract nor concrete, neither rational nor irrational, neither real nor unreal. *Imaginatio* is both: it is the aristocratic preoccupation of one who is set apart, chosen, predestined by God from the very beginning.[56]

In order for Henderson to open the door, to find that key to the mystery of his existence, he had to experience the "preoccupation of *one* who is set apart (separated), chosen and predestined from the beginning."[57] He had to really listen to the voice of his soul and seek direction from *it*, instead of his ego.

In Jungian terms the inner friend who goes with us everywhere can be found in our dreams, fantasies, and by means of active imagination. That is the way to the Self, not "doing" something. For all the things Henderson did, all the possessions he owned, and that includes his possessive attitude towards his wives and his children, in the end none of them led him anywhere.

By the end of the book he is left with only himself and a tiny lion cub he has snatched from the village. He believes that this tiny cub contains the spirit of his dead friend, the king. It is his need to sustain contact with that aspect of the Self that makes him take the cub. He needs to remember that experience.

The final scene in the book finds Henderson on an airplane going home to America. He is a changed man, now sensitive and kind. He meets an orphan on board, a foreign child who has just lost his parents, and is drawn to him. Earlier, at the beginning of his story before he came to Africa, he encounters an orphan and is so repelled that he refuses to come out of his room until the child is gone. But as I said, he has changed and is different.

He wraps the child in a blanket when the plane lands for refueling in Newfoundland. He holds him close to his chest and thinks to himself that "he is like medicine applied." And then he says, "The great beautiful propellers are still, all four of them. I guess it was my turn now to move

---

56 Jung, "Projection of Psychic Content," CW 12, ¶¶ 400-401.
57 Jung, "Projection of Psychic Content," CW 12, ¶¶ 400-401.

and so I went running, leaping, pounding and tingling over the pure white lining of the gray arctic silence."[58]

To be reunited with the Self, to meet the king, to know the orphan, the undivided one that brings energy, renewal and meaning to life, and to be victorious over chaos . . . what more could anyone ask?

---

58 Bellow, *Henderson the Rain King*, 341.

Chapter 5

IMAGE AND IMAGINATION
WOUNDING AND HEALING

From a Presentation to the Oregon Friends of Jung[59]

There is an old Hindu legend about Brahma. Brahma was sitting around with his disciples and decided to take away man's divine power. There was a time when all men were like gods, but they had abused that divinity and the Chief God, Brahma, was going to hide it where man would never find it again. "Should we put it into the depths of the ocean, or into the depths of the earth or the heights of the heavens?" they wondered. But with each suggestion they agreed that man was curious and might some day go up or down or into these realms. So they decided to hide it where man would never look. Brahma said: "Here is what we will do with man's divinity. We will hide it deep within man himself for he will never think to look for it there."

The legend goes on to say that ever since man has been going up and down the earth, climbing, digging, diving, exploring, searching for something that is already in himself.

I feel that way about play, about the imagination, about the creative within us all. When I use the word *imagination*, *play*, or *creative*, I mean all three: I interchange them because play and creativity have to go together and be joined by the imagination.

If you are playing with an idea, you are in a creative process or playing with a fantasy. I don't mean Disneyland-like play. That isn't the kind of

---

59 Gilda Frantz, "Image and Imagination; Wounding and Healing," (from audiocassette recording of presentation to Oregon Friends of Jung, #134).

play that will change your life. But if you have read *Memories, Dreams, Reflections*, you recall Jung's purposeful play. It begins with his recollecting about his school years:

> School came to bore me. It took up far too much time which I would rather have spent drawing battles and playing with fire. . . . I was exempted from drawing classes on grounds of utter incapacity . . . it was another defeat, since I had some facility in drawing but I could only draw what stirred my imagination. . . . I was forced to copy prints of Greek Gods with sightless eyes and when that wouldn't go properly . . . I failed completely and that was the end of my drawing classes.[60]

In a later chapter on "Confrontation with the Unconscious," Jung writes of a time when he was under constant pressure after his break with Freud:

> Since I *know nothing at all* (isn't that true despair when we are in a place of knowing nothing at all?), I shall do whatever occurs to me; thus I consciously submitted myself to the impulses of the unconscious. The first thing that came to the surface was a childhood memory from perhaps my 10th year. At that time I was passionate about playing with building blocks. I distinctly recalled how I had built little houses and castles, using bottles to form the sides of gates and vaults ... to my astonishment this memory was accompanied by a good deal of emotion. Aha! I said, there is still life in these things. The small boy is still around and possesses a creative life which I lack. But how can I make my way to it?[61]

He continues:

> For as a grown man it seemed impossible to me that I should be able to bridge the distance from the present back to my 11th year. Yet, if I wanted to re-establish contact with that period, I had no choice but to return to it and take up once

---

60 C.G. Jung, *MDR*, 27-29.
61 Jung, *MDR*, 173-174, emphasis added.

more that child's life with his childish games. *This moment was a turning point in my fate*, but I gave in only after endless resistances and with a sense of resignation. For it was a painfully humiliating experience to realize that there was nothing to be done except play childish games.[62]

He then recounts how he built cottages, a castle, an entire village, and a church. He played every day after lunch and when he had time to spare (he continued to see patients): "For the building/game was only a beginning. It released a stream of fantasies which I later carefully wrote down."[63]

This play of Jung's was serious and purposeful. After thinking about Jung's recollection of his school years, I looked up the word *recollect*. It means to gather, and following that a bit further, I found that it comes from the same root word as *good*. So, the recollecting, the gathering in, the remembering is holy work.

It was that for a woman who after many years of analysis recalled a painful time in her childhood when she was new in the neighborhood and without friends. She was alone during the day while her mother worked and, being 9 or 10, still not allowed to cook on the stove when alone. So, she made up an alchemical game. She would go into the kitchen and grind up various grains, each separately and in its own bowl. Then, carefully measuring a pinch of this, a half teaspoon of that, she would concoct what would be the perfect food that would save the world from starvation. Only the tiniest amount of this would be sufficient to nourish the person for the entire day. This game was played, she said, in absolute secrecy and always alone. No one ever knew she did this. This simple childhood game was a healing use of the imagination because the child was not being nourished; her personal parents weren't able to give her the spiritual food she needed and the psyche was showing her that she had the ability to provide that nourishment out of her own imagination.

Dreams and fantasies are the most powerful and present manifestations of the creative imagination we have. The imagination is the

---

62 Jung, *MDR*, 174, emphasis added.
63 Jung, *MDR*, 175.

Royal Road toward wholeness. In dreams and fantasies the imagination is unfettered and free. In Jung's words: "Each new day, reality is created by the psyche. . . . Fantasy is the creative activity whence issue the *solutions to all answerable questions*; it is the mother of all possibilities, in which too, the inner and outer worlds, like all psychological antithesis, are joined in living union."[64] The game the woman played, recalled from childhood, was such a re-creating of each day. Each of you has tucked away some such recollection from childhood, which has survived unscathed. No doubt secret games are psyche's insurance that certain healing and golden imaginings from childhood survive and can be recalled like Jung's game.

In the June 1980 issue of *New Realities* magazine, edited by James Bolen of San Franciso, there is an angry article by Marilyn Ferguson entitled "Humanizing Learning."

She says that just as in medical iatrogenic (doctor-caused) illnesses, we have the equivalent in schools of teacher-caused learning disabilities. In contrast to insects, human beings start out as butterflies and end up in cocoons!!!

During the years I spent working in clay, mid-wifing the birth of the imagination in wounded adults, I heard many horror stories about school-related injuries to the imaginative, creative side. As a child's young foot can be deformed by being forced to wear too tight shoes, a too restrictive attitude on the part of any authority can be wounding to the imagination. When an injury occurs to this symbol-forming part of ourselves, the drawing, doodling, spontaneous part, something stops. Like a sea anemone, when touched harshly, it pulls into itself.

The tragedy of the wound to the symbol-making energy within is that it can stop suddenly, and very few adults notice its absence. Part of that has to do with our culture and its focus on the intellect and rational products. Children rarely have to be told to draw—it is a natural activity. Someone said that creativity is observable in all children and a few adults. We place little value on the *work* of the imagination. The so-called childish play, like Jung's building blocks, and the woman's alchemy game were vital, instinctive activities of the unconscious, done

---

64 C.G. Jung, "The Type Problem in Classical and Medival Thought," CW 6, ¶ 78, emphasis added.

in secret away from the all too critical eye of parents and teachers. Susan Bach, a London analyst, has studied the paintings of terminally ill children for years and has developed the hypothesis that in those drawings the child unconsciously paints, in symbolic terms, the exact time left to live. That astounding fact shows how serious and deep and knowing is children's play.

I've heard stories about teachers tearing up pictures because a sky was painted black by a depressed child or hanging all the pictures but one for an open house. And so on. I always wondered what it was that had caused these individuals *never* to use nonverbal means again to express their imagination. They were/are normal, neurotic people and yet when these childhood traumas were recollected, they said they never again touched paints, crayons, or clay. How many of you can recall a *moment* when such an event happened? I think that it wasn't just the act of criticizing the painting or tearing it up that was crucial. It was the symbol being expressed that was torn up, maimed and hurt. Not the clay or paper—the *symbol* and its rich meaning.

If you can recall what you were making just before you never drew again, that memory would enable you to *recollect*, to gather it to yourself and begin to heal that wounding to your ability to express your symbolic life nonverbally.

Children do not draw just for the hell of it. Drawing, clay modeling, and such are deeply serious activities of the psyche in the service of expressing the *unexpressable*.

Jung observed his inner child and listened to what that child wanted to do—humiliating as this felt for a scientist to do. From this sprang "active imagination"—that bridge between conscious and unconscious, between outer and inner realms. Children *live* in the realm of the archetypes, the imagination, and are in communication with it—a realm most adults forget about until something gathers together memories of the past—needed as healing energies for the present. In *Psychological Types* Jung said: "This autonomous activity of the psyche . . . is like every vital process a continually creative act. The psyche creates reality every day. . . . Fantasy is the clearest expression of the psyche."[65]

---

65 C.G. Jung, "The Type Problem," CW 6, ¶ 78.

In *Woman's Mysteries*, Esther Harding says that each of us has within us a creator and that our task in life is to allow ourselves to create something that did not exist before—not a product, but to experience what it is to take raw material, that is, life, and by breathing our life into it we can make it a living creation. This unfolds the power of the creator who sleeps within all of us. She calls this our *most* "God-like faculty."

Recollecting is a way of gathering the raw material of life, isn't it? This God-like faculty is our imagination, for in the imagination anything is possible. I see that when the symbol is torn up, derided or ignored, something occurs which possibly ceases to allow us to trust that nonverbal expression or maybe even to trust the symbol-maker itself.

In a study on mourning and grieving it was shown that the loss of a loved one is not dissimilar to the loss of an arm or leg. What kind of grieving takes place in the loss of nonverbal expression through trauma? I wonder. Are our lives still being dictated by the all-too-critical judgments of an inner authority? Do we carry within us an introjected critical authority that doesn't *allow* the inner creator expression? Or spontaneity? The results of this wounding to the symbol-making part of us can be depression, feelings of unworthiness, ugliness, low self-esteem, stuckness.

Now, much of what I have said isn't new at all, especially to artists, writers, and inventors. They welcome the tension they experience in the creative process because they know that it is necessary and vital. In *Courage to Create*, Rollo May says that it takes courage to face the unknown.

Our imagination is a God-given gift, as much a part of us as is walking, talking, seeing, or hearing. Actually, it is more related to communication. Some children develop a large vocabulary early in their new lives and other children learn to speak later—but if we learn to speak, we expect to do so all of our lives. So it is with the imagination. If it is unimpaired by outside influences, we are able to express ourselves nonverbally or verbally all of our lives, into adulthood and old age. But many of us aren't able to put pencil to paper. We say: "I don't know how; I can't draw; I'm not talented; my sister/brother is the artist in our family."

The late Hilde Kirsch said that she would be happy if children were not graded for artwork, that the use of the imagination should not be competitive. I think of the man whose painting wasn't chosen to hang with others in his class. In his case, the teacher's oversight effectively told him he was unworthy, inferior. The fact that the product of his imagination was rejected was like she had rejected him, and he never painted again until middle-age.

When I say *creative*, I don't mean *talent*. Although each of us is creative, or potentially so, only a few possess talent. Yet, these two words are often linked to our misfortune. I like to think of creativity as cre*ac*tivity—an energy, if you will.

J.D. Salinger would be an example of large talent, low creativity. Picasso was enormously creactive as well as talented. By the way, Picasso used to say that his paintings didn't show what he was *looking for*, but what he *found*. Rollo May thinks of Thomas Wolfe as a man of enormous creative energy, but small talent.

Ordinary adults who present themselves to a lump of clay suffer the humiliation to the ego Jung spoke of earlier, and experience what the neglected creative imagination desires.

One older woman learned to love her short, squat hands by using them in the service of the creative. Before, she hated them. But after her experience in which they had become instruments of the creative spirit, they became beautiful to her. She had come to this artwork in a severe depression over the loss of a loved one, and yet she tended to deprecate what she made and to joke about the figures. One day her hands touched the clay and there appeared a tall, graceful woman with arms cradling—emptiness. The old woman began to cry and out came some tragic event in her life. But the really important fact was that she began to have a feeling of self-worth through by actively participating in the process of recollection.

She told me a story. "I was a curious child," she said, "who used to tell fantastic stories. My mother could never tell if the stories were true or not. I was often left alone with Mother when Father went off to work and my sisters went off to school. One day I was sitting by the window and saw a hunch-back with a small hump on his back, his thin body like a stick.

"To me, his face had a dark look. I ran to my mother and asked, 'Why does that man look like that? What made him look like that?' My mother looked at him and then at me. 'That man looks like that,' she said, 'because there is a little man who sits on his hump. Whenever the man wants to eat food, the little man on his hump grabs it. That's why he is so thin. The reason he has a hump is because he told stories as a child that were not always true.'

"So," said this woman, "I stopped telling stories altogether." And for most of her life she found that the only food that nourished her was put into her mouth instead of her imagination. A theft is taking place of which many of us are unaware. I am referring, of course, to the theft of the imaginative faculty in childhood.

I would like to share a recollection from my own childhood. I think it is my first experience with the creative imagination. I was around 4½ or 5 years old and staying with relatives for a long visit, which lasted a year. Early on, I began to have nightmares due to this early separation from the mother. One night I found a solution that helped. Just before falling asleep I would visualize a large picture book. I would turn the pages of this huge book until a pleasant picture appeared, quickly flipping past scary ones. When I settled on a good picture, that would be the beginning of my dream.

This ritual was psyche's creative, imaginative way of helping me deal with a painful separation. Also, it was, like the woman's alchemy game, a solution that came from the inner realm, thus giving courage and strength to a young ego.

Attempting to write this article, I felt identical with the wounded aspect of the imagination—the topic. My offering seemed too small, insignifcant, unworthy. The colors too dull, too dry for so large a canvas—and too few. When that happens I feel that I am in a desert; there is no revivifying water in my soul and the fear of failure grips me.

My own woundedness is why I am speaking to you on this subject. We all speak out of our own wounds. Some of us become submerged in the damned-up waters and are stuck there, full of soul, full of juice, potential, but "something" keeps us from contact with it. I do not speak of products here, but process. It is not products *per se* that the imagination needs, but often it is in the products of its creactivity that we see its existence and know its presence.

The imagination is as vast as the unconscious itself and thus is the perfect instrument or medium by which we meet the unconscious and in which healing can take place. As homeopaths say: "Like heals like." If the injury is to the imaginative faculty, then the imaginative faculty will be the source of the healing. The alchemical saying is that what has been wounded by the father can only be healed by the father. The unlimited, unfettered symbol-making, image-making imagination is the tincture needed to heal the wound.

In childhood we are so close to the unconscious and the imaginal realm, we offer its products as sweet fruits to those near us. Expressing this realm nonverbally in drawings is a natural instinctive activity of the psyche. Children have direct access to symbols. Therapists who work imaginally with children know how quickly some children can respond to the healing, ordering principle of the images in sandplay or other play therapy techniques.

Jung called his most important tool "active imagination," signifying that there needs to be an active participation between the inner and outer realms, between ego and archetype. It is like two lovers. When they engage actively in making love, when it is mutual—when the desire is equally intense on both parts—it is always a numinous experience.

This creactivity of ego and archetype is where one meets the regal nature of the imagination. Jung says the alchemists called imagination the most important key to the understanding of the opus. Could we say less?

The resistance we all feel toward "play" is in itself often the motivating force in our lives. Like those of us who have experienced *any* sort of addiction, the person who avoids the playful, imaginal instinct thinks about nothing else! The starved soul is always sighing within us, hoping we hear her sighs and give her what she yearns for. Instead, we obsessively think about not doing or compare what we could do to the inferior products of someone whose creativity isn't hampered by a labyrinth-like approach. The labyrinth is, in fact, an excellent image for the lost imagination. Most of us are unaware of an Ariadne who can lead our imaginal selves out of the depth of the unconscious into the light of new consciousness.

Another misconception of the play instinct is that what the imagination produces must be "useful" in some way. It may be, but its "usefulness" may not be evident in our lives for years. What a pity to squelch that fire because our puny conscious attitude can't find a "use" for it at once. Look at the image and perhaps a new *usefulness* may emerge. Are dreams *useful?*

There is in us a child quality that *needs* to create simple things that have never been before, and too often we bring an all-too-critical attitude to imaginal work and kill it before it has had a chance to emerge. The first time I worked in clay as an adult had a transforming effect upon me. I felt more than I was before, a person I had always yearned to be. In the moment I touched the clay I had an intimation of something very much greater than what had been before.

I cannot stress enough how important it is to allow yourself to do something that you have never done before and that you aren't "good" at. Most of us spend ourselves doing what the ego does best, because the little ego doesn't like to take a back seat—ever.

When we do this, we meet the numinosity that brings a new spiritual meaning to all of our lives.

> Clay is not necessarily
> for everyone—it is
> just what I like.
> Poetry sculpting, singing
> —dance movement.

Mind/Brain Bulletin reported research on the use of imagination in enhancing learning. If children act out fairy tales, they develop greater cognitive ability! I wonder what would happen to adults if we allowed our imagination a place in our lives? Would our cognitive ability improve?

Erich Neumann's *Art and the Creative Unconscious* is a real gold mine. "Domination by our one-sided culture of consciousness has let the individual almost to a sclerosis of consciousness; he has become well-incapable of psychic transformation. In this situation the ego becomes an exclusive ego, a development reflected in such terms as 'egotistic' and 'egocentric.'"[66] It follows that *openness makes the child receptive to suffering and experience.* It is this attitude that you must bring to a lump of clay or a sheet of paper. It isn't easy to face the void, the unknown, but often worthwhile. The suffering can be used and experienced.

Neumann says that the history of every creative person is always close to the abyss of sickness. Creative people do not, as do others, tend to heal personal wounds by increased adaptivity. These wounds remain open, but their suffering is situated in depths from which another curative power arises—and this curative power is the creative process. Being connected to the imaginal realm can be healing. The artist *uses* his or her suffering, whereas most of us try to avoid it. The expression of our imagination defines us.

I found a poem written by an unknown poet: "The sky and earth are *born* of my own eyes, hard and soft, cold and hot are the products of my own body—the perfume and the odor are in my own nose." And a poem by a 30-year-old man about his first experience with clay:

> Today I touched the soul—hard-soft, damp/dry heavy form yielding to me. I'm a child. Feel the dirt, the earth—the mud. The kid is at home, thank God. All man's imagination indwells. Squeeze, knead, coax. What will release—be released, be born?

This is just a part of his poem, but I think it says perfectly what I am trying to convey. It is not the expression of great beauty that we are looking for but an expression of our innermost soul.

While thinking about this presentation, I played with clay and what emerged was a fantastic creature giving birth to eggs—through her mouth! She was a prehistoric reptilian manifestation of the unconscious. One egg had hatched already revealing an adorable replica of Mama, while another rested in her mouth waiting to be born. She personified the imagination to me, life-giving and unique. It was something that "I"

---

66 Erich Neumann, *Art and the Creative Unconscious*, 160.

as ego could have never have thought of; such archaic images lie deep within waiting for release.

Artists create because they must, not because they want to. They really don't have a choice; they are possessed by a daimon. Kieffer Frantz wrote a paper on healing in which he mentioned the saving qualities of reconnecting to the creative imagination. Dashiel Hammett, Anthony Burgess, and Sam Francis were three examples he used.

Dashiel Hammett was given six months to live and thought, "Hell, if I'm going to die, I might just as well quit this stupid job and do what I've always wanted to do"—which was write a book. He died many years later. Anthony Burgess was given a year to live and he, too, reacted in a similar way—and is still alive. Sam Francis was dying and in a hospital, and was given a small box of paints—and he painted himself well! Each of these are examples of the solution found within the person, similar to Norman Cousins' imaginative solutions to his own serious illness. The solution to the problem, like our divinity, comes from within. The curative power of the imagination is within.

Injuries to the creative imagination create in us a reluctance to touch that part again. Francis Wickes, in her book *The Inner World of Childhood*, speaks to the difference in the introverted and extraverted child. The example she uses has to do with the relationship each has to the object. If the teacher of an introverted child, while being helpful with an art or craft assignment touches the child's work in any way, the child might say or think "now it isn't mine any more," *whereas* the extraverted child will happily accept the help and thank the teacher. This relation to the object would make it vital for parents and teachers of introverts to understand this special relationship to the object and help them keep their hands (or comments) off the child's products. I think that introverted children are more prone both to express the symbolic image early on *and* to receive a wound early on, also. I think what Francis Wickes was saying is that extraverts adapt more easily to outer change. Introverted children find that more difficult. I'm talking about respecting human efforts. Expand the possibilities, don't limit them.

Marie-Louise von Franz says that people often resist becoming creative because one's *would-be* creativeness is always so much more impressive than the little egg one lays in the end. She says the mountain brings forth a mouse—but maybe it was more than a mouse.

Expression, Repression, Depression

If we repress the images that yearn for expression, then psyche creates a depression to reconnect us with the depths, the underworld, so we can see what strange, mysterious stuff is within. Esther Harding speaks of this process in *The Value and Meaning of Depression*. When you sit down with your clay or drawing materials, you are bringing symbols to birth.

Jung says the chief value of these images is in assuring subjective happiness and well-being irrespective of the changing aspects of outer reality. You feel better when you allow your imagination a chance to play. Jung says, "The goal of life is not perfection but completeness."[67] Hopefully, we will all find it.

---

67   C.G. Jung, CW 12, ¶ 208.

Part 2

MYSTERIOUS WORKINGS OF THE PSYCHE

No one develops his personality because somebody tells him that it would be useful or advisable to do so. Nature has never yet been taken in by well-meaning advice. The only thing that moves nature is causal necessity, and that goes for human nature too. Without necessity nothing budges, the human personality least of all. It is tremendously conservative, not to say torpid. Only acute necessity is able to rouse it. The developing personality obeys no caprice, no command, no insight, only brute necessity; it needs the motivating force of inner or outer fatalities. Any other development would be no better than individualism. That is why the cry of "individualism" is a cheap insult when flung at the natural development of personality.

—C.G. Jung[68]

---

68   C.G. Jung, "The Development of Personality," CW 17, ¶ 293.

Chapter 6

DREAMS AND SUDDEN DEATH

Originally published in *The Dream and Its Amplification*[69]

> He looked at his own Soul
> With a Telescope. What seemed
> All irregular, he saw and
> Shewed to be beautiful
> Constellations; and he added
> To the Consciousness hidden
> Worlds within worlds.
> —Samuel Taylor Coleridge, *Notebooks*[70]

It has been my unique experience to have witnessed the sudden death of several beloved family members. After my husband's totally unexpected death, when I was only in my late forties, I was eaten up by loneliness. For months I felt as though the house had a zipper that shut me out of life and kept life out of my home. I lived in the realm of the dead. It was then, in my sadness and pain, that I thought of my husband's dream journal. We were an inseparable couple, but both of us were extremely private people who had never looked at the other's dream journal or peeked into anything private. Now there I was, a bereft widow yearning for my husband, drawn toward taking a liberty I never would have imagined. Only after I spoke with his spirit and asked permission was

---

69 Gilda Frantz, "Dreams and Sudden Death" in *The Dream and Its Amplification*, 205–214.

70 As cited in C.G. Jung, *MDR*.

I able to open his dream book. I turned to my own dreams at the same time and discovered a unique record in the dreams he'd dreamt not long before he died and in my dreams from about two months before that.

This article is culled from my personal experience. Because it is personal, I took the advice of the ancient alchemists, who noted that there comes a time when one must throw away the books. This important statement has guided me to consider the dream and my own process rather than to pour over books to validate what I have written.

What now seems like a lifetime ago, the dream I had about two months before my husband's "sudden" death was a puzzle to me because I forgot the most important associations when I attempted to analyze it. The memory of two significant dreams that might have clarified the subject of this particular dream came later. It also appears that, unsurprisingly, I was very resistant to becoming conscious of the fact that my husband, Kieffer, was going to die soon. In *On Dreams and Death*, von Franz writes: "In cases where the dreamer has illusions about his approaching death or is unaware of its closeness, dreams may even indicate this fact quite brutally and mercilessly."[71] I think the dream I had was fairly blunt, but I just didn't get it at the time.

This dream came at a very happy time in my life. I had been in the training program of the Jung Institute of Los Angeles for two years, and for the first time in decades I had time for myself and was enjoying the freedom as well as the studies. As our children were grown, my husband and I began having dinner dates after work, and life was good. Into my happy life came this dream:

> *I am part of a very large group of people from my neighborhood who were running down the street as if to get away from a catastrophe. We are all terrorized. As I run, I look up the hill on my right and see my home. A huge bank of earth has fallen away, and I think, "This cleft in the earth has changed the landscape." I repeated this thought to a person who was running by my side: "Because of this catastrophe, the landscape will never be the same again. It has changed forever."*

---

71 Marie-Louise von Franz, *On Dreams and Death*, ix.

When I awoke, I had no idea what the catastrophe might be. The word *catastrophe* means a great and sudden calamity, a disaster. It was only much later that I recalled waking up on the morning of June 6, 1961, and finding out that Jung had died. My dream from that night: *A huge bank of earth had broken away from behind the pool area and dropped down into the pool.*

At my analytical appointment I told my analyst the dream and wondered aloud what the Jungian world would be like with Jung gone. Her reply was interesting. She said that probably male analysts who didn't feel they'd had a chance to be seen or heard while Jung lived, would now have that opportunity. It felt clear in the dream that Jung and his work had dropped down to an even deeper place.

In another dream, also dreamt in the early 1960s, I saw a huge owl land in our front yard. When I awoke from the dream in the middle of the night, I actually could hear an owl hooting. I then learned that my sister-in-law had died in a plane crash on her flight from New York. In my associations to this dream I learned that the owl is a bird associated with death. After I remembered my associations, I thought that my dream of a catastrophe might mean that someone had died, but there was no news of that, so my dream remained a puzzle. It just never occurred to me that my dream might be *pointing to a death to come.* I think it is clear that I didn't want to see what the dream was telling me.

About a month or two after I had this dream, my husband died suddenly at home, without illness or any warning. With all the shock and confusion sudden death brings, it took quite awhile for me to remember the dream. One day some time later, I was taking a walk early in the morning when the memory of the dream became conscious and I realized that I was now living what the dream had referred to: My own earth had been changed by what now really was a catastrophic loss for me. When the memory of the dream came back to me, it also brought back what my husband was doing when he died. We were outside on a beautiful, sunny day, and he was repotting a small azalea plant that he felt needed to be in a larger-sized pot; its current pot was crowding the azalea's growth.

We in the Western world view death as a catastrophe or a tragedy. In the East there is more of a sense of destiny and fulfillment that comes with death. There is sadness, of course, but also acceptance of the continuation of one's journey. Holy men and women meditate for years to achieve within themselves what is a peaceful attitude toward that which is inevitable. We in the West say, for example, "He put up a *good fight*" or "She was ill for years and finally *succumbed after a long battle.*" I think many in the East surrender to death when it feels right to do so and die with an understanding that they are continuing their journey. This is especially likely in cultures in which reincarnation is seen as a means of possibly improving one's karma in the next life. I think that most cultures see death as an end to suffering.

One thing I never wanted to say about my husband's death was that it was tragic. It wasn't. I subscribed to the ancient Greek way of looking at tragedy. Death wasn't considered tragic unless there had been waste involved. My husband had lived a full life. He was a physician who was gifted in treating mental illness. He helped found the Society of Jungian Analysts and the Los Angeles Institute that bears Jung's name. He was director of the first low-fee adult clinic that offered Jungian analysis to those who could not afford private care. That clinic now is named after him, the Kieffer E. Frantz Clinic. And, he practiced meditation for over 30 years. He was a loving father to his two children. No waste here that I could see—although *I* felt cheated that he had died at what seemed to me to be so young an age.

My husband's dream journals now gave me great comfort; he had spent much time in this endeavor of writing down his dreams. I also read the active imaginations he did around his dreams. I looked to see what his dreams were saying before he died and found that he, too, was getting dreams about something foreboding.

> Kieffer's dream: *Gilda and I are driving into a desert from which no one returns. There were eleven-legged wolves there.*

I could see from his handwriting that this dream made a huge impression on him. He devoted a great deal of time writing about the dream and researching its symbols. He noted that often St. Paul was referred to as a wolf. His active imagination with his anima made it clear that he saw the dream as a warning about death and that he needed help from the archetypal figures in the unconscious to help him deal with this threat to his being. But with all this insight, he also made a note that he thought he would live another ten years.

It feels to me that the unconscious tries to shake us up and wake us up, but some of us have resistance to taking in information that we deem to be scary, unpleasant, or a threat to our status quo. That was true of my husband and true of myself. Neither of us could take in that our dreams were saying that life as we knew it was ending or was about to change dramatically.

In *Body and Soul* by Albert Kreinheder, I recall that he reported a dream in which he was digging his own grave. When he awoke, he felt that the dream was telling him to get his affairs in order. This would be an example of a blunt dream in which the unconscious senses the dreamer's resistance to death. The dream makes it clear that it's not far off. The dream my late husband had may have been that kind of dream. His dream made him aware of his vulnerability. He took the dream about going to a desert from which no one returned seriously, talking with his anima about wolves and sheep. He "talked" with St. Paul, invoking him to do something about the wolves that were howling. So I know how much he took the idea of death seriously, but since he was well and only in his early sixties, he just couldn't believe that it was his time to die. But it was.

Many years later I was in Greece on a tour with the philosopher Betty Smith when I had another dream about a catastrophe. It happened that I was doing research on The Fates, so being in Greece was the perfect environment in which to find out more about these goddesses. I traveled all over Greece and saw statuary of the gods and goddesses in museums and temples. I totally fell in love with this magical place where Western civilization began. One night I had this dream:

> *I am in Greece, swimming in the clear blue water of a small inlet dedicated to Demeter, and there are only a few people in the water, three or four. My back is to the ocean and I am facing the shore, which is near. I turn around and look out to sea and*

notice a huge wall of water at a great distance. It is a tsunami.
I look away again and the next thing I know, the wall of water
is above me and momentarily will crash down upon my head. I
think, "No one can survive this catastrophe."

In thinking about this dream, I thought that "this catastrophe" might not be personal but instead referring to a coming world catastrophe. When I looked up through the wall of water, I could see the sun through the blue-green flourescent water. That might indicate spiritual light, not obliteration.

The next time I thought of the dream I was at a cemetery attending the funeral of my little granddaughter. When I recalled the dream, I grabbed a friend's arm and whispered that now I understood what the dream meant. While I was in Greece I could not stop thinking of my granddaughter and buying her little trinkets. She was always on my mind.

Demeter is the Great Mother. Her daughter Persephone was taken from her by Hades. He carried Persephone down to the Underworld, where she became queen. At the time of her rape by Hades she was a Kore, a very young child/woman. Demeter worshipped her daughter and went into mourning at her disappearance, refusing to allow anything to grow, as she was the goddess who ruled the growth of grains and plants and life itself. She dressed in black and became a nursemaid to a mortal child, attempting to make him immortal by holding him over a fire every evening. She was discovered and forced to leave. The child survived but never became immortal. Persephone pleaded with her brother Zeus to make Hades give her daughter back to her, which Zeus tried to do. They worked out an arrangement where Persephone stayed with her mother in spring and summer and returned to Hades and the Underworld in fall and winter. Thus, the myth goes, that is why the leaves die on the trees and nothing grows when Persephone remains in Hades during those months.

Seeing the setting in Greece and especially in a body of water sacred to Demeter, the dream seemed to place the catastrophe in the realm of the Great Mother. This dream seemed to tell me something huge was about to inundate my ego, and once more I used the word *catastro-*

phe, that sudden calamity from which no one can survive. And when my grandchild was being buried, going down into the Underworld of Hades, I remembered the dream.

Our dreams of death or near-death signify that these deaths have meaning for us. They are not simply *sudden*—as in *unexpected*—but have much deeper roots in our souls, and their coming is already known in the unconscious and therefore expected.

In an auditory vision a voice told me that people don't just die, they are *called*, and when they hear this *call*, they leave. It feels to me that my late husband was called and that my granddaughter was called, and that is how I explain sudden death. I cannot even ask the question of why we are sent these dreams to help us become conscious of a mystical experience that is about to envelop us. When Jung was asked if he believed in God, his answer was, "I don't believe, I know." I feel that way about such dreams. I know that they are trying to help us prepare for this mystical and profound loss.

I think that it is important to look at a dream as a mystery—a mystery that uses symbolic language and that is necessary to solve. Dreams can be extremely mysterious. One might even say they are veiled, elusive, and often hard to grasp. We need to work to understand our dreams, although we all know of the experience of awaking from a dream and suddenly realizing what it is about. But that doesn't happen very often. More common is the experience of waking up with the mists of the unconscious still clinging to our nightclothes and our head feeling heavy and our eyes unable to fully open to the day. These are the times when the unconscious won't easily let go of us. Some dreamers awake this way daily and others of us occasionally, but it is an experience many of us have had.

But we have something besides our dreams to guide us here as well. A couple of months before my husband died, and around the time I had the dream of running from a catastrophe, my husband said goodbye to me as he departed for a one-week retreat to the mountains to study healing, a subject in which he was profoundly interested. I found myself alone in our home for the first time ever. My children were in college, and there I was in a huge home by myself. One evening I was sitting in front of the fire, my feet on the raised brick hearth. Our dog Pepper was at my feet and our big tomcat Eli in my lap.

My journal was open, as I had been writing in it. I closed my eyes and thought: "If I were to be widowed, this is how my life would be. I would be alone with my dog and cat as companions."

I had never thought about this possibility before in this way because I'd always had my children to care for when my husband went to conferences. Even though I had resisted the idea of my dream signifying something to do with death, my soul understood and tried, through a seemingly innocuous thought, to impart this information to me. The memory of this thought, much later on, helped me cope with being a widow. Something deep within me was directing my footsteps onto a new path during that week alone, and it saved my life. I did not become bitter when my husband died, leaving me alone in my late forties. I didn't know it, but I had been prepared. The unconscious understands that we can resist or fail to understand dream messages, so it sends us thoughts in our waking life to nudge us toward consciousness. Somehow I could accept the visual scene of sitting with my pets, alone in a big house, better than a dream about catastrophe. The two occasions worked together to bring me consciousness in however long it took for me to "get it."

The work of C.G. Jung and his colleague Marie-Louise von Franz has illuminated the world of dreams and the unconscious so that we know it is a part of us that is real, that we exist in both inner and outer worlds. That famous story of Jung describing a woman's dream of being on the moon to von Franz when she first met Jung comes to mind. He said that the dreamer was *on* the moon and von Franz interrupted, saying, you mean she *dreamt* she was on the moon, and Jung said, no, she *was on* the moon.

That is how real the unconscious is. I believe that these dreams and thoughts are gifts from the unconscious to bring me the understanding that the sudden deaths I witnessed in loved ones were not sudden after all but were known in the unconscious, and that I was being informed that something momentous and life-changing was about to happen that would affect me profoundly.

When writing a long letter, many of us add a postscript to include a thought that has been left out. I often do, and I feel the need to do so today after rereading this article. I can see that my intuitive–feeling nature has not done a great job of explaining the leap I made from having a dream to concluding that it was a warning about death. What I neglected to explain is how I made that leap. Intuition often does that; it leaps and hurls itself across vast chasms, just because it "feels right." I have had a lifetime of dream interpretation in my practice with others and with myself. Sometimes a feeling simply tells me that what I am feeling is so. Others may not see it that way, but it satisfies me.

In the event that you have a complex dream, you must have someone listen to it and help you understand what the dream is saying. It is better not to leap to conclusions unless that has been the way you access knowledge and have spent a lifetime doing it. The most important thing to do with a dream is to write down all you can recall about it and then write down all of your associations to the elements in the dream. Remember at the early part of this article, I noted that I didn't recall an event when I was gathering associations, and that if I had, I would have better understood the dream? And sooner understood the dream? That is how important associations are. As an introverted intuitive with extraverted feeling (to use the parlance of Jung's typology), I am used to listening to my intuitions and feelings. That is how I drew the conclusions I did, through strong feelings and strong intuitions.

Chapter 7

CREATIVITY AND INSPIRATION:
AN INTERVIEW WITH STEPHEN MARTIN

Originally published in *Psychological Perspectives*[72]

I am speaking with Dr. Stephen Martin on the phone, as he is in the Philadelphia area and I am in Santa Monica. He is sitting in his library at home, a room filled with the evidence of his many interests: shelves stacked with books about the decorative arts of the twentieth century; examples of that work in silver and enamel; paintings commissioned from artist friends; and a collection of letters, manuscripts, photographs, and volumes all inscribed or signed by C.G. Jung.

Dr. Martin is a clinical psychologist and Jungian analyst. A graduate of the C.G. Jung Institute in Zürich, he completed his training in 1980 when he was quite young. He is the editor of the definitive monograph on Archibald Knox, one of the most important British decorative artists of the twentieth century, as well as the former editor-in-chief of *Quadrant*, our sister publication. He co-hosted, with Aryeh Maidenbaum, the groundbreaking conference in the late 1980s on Jung and anti-Semitism and coedited with him the sourcebook on that subject, *Lingering Shadows: Jungians, Freudians and Anti-Semitism*, which has recently been reissued. He is co-founder and President Emeritus of the Philemon Foundation. With the recent publication of *The Red Book* and the extensive coverage of this event by the *New York Times* and news media around the world, the Philemon Foundation, which funded much of

---

72 Gilda Frantz, "Creativity and Inspiration: An Interview with Stephen Martin," *Psychological Perspectives* 53(4), (2010): 396-409.

The Red Book's editorial preparation and all of its translation, has been a very visible institution indeed. As president, Dr. Martin sought and secured the funds needed for the editorial preparation of *The Red Book* as well as for other publications funded by the Philemon Foundation, including the *Jung-White Letters*, published by Routledge, and Jung's *Seminar on Children's Dreams*, published by Princeton University Press. Since its publication in October 2009 by W.W. Norton, *The Red Book* has become a sensation in the book world, with its initial print run of 5,000 copies selling out almost before its publication date. Subsequent printings have been selling briskly. The enormous popularity of *The Red Book* was no surprise to Steve Martin, given that it was his inner certainty of its vital importance to the world that brought him to establish the Philemon Foundation in the first place.

> Gilda Frantz (GF): Steve, how did you come to create this foundation?

> Stephen Martin (SM): *Creation* is really the right word here because the foundation was born in an unpremeditated instant, a creative moment, coming to me unbidden at the end of what was quite a casual lunchtime conversation with Sonu Shamdasani on July 4, 2003. I was visiting London, having planned the trip months before to pick up some letters by Jung to H. G. Baynes that I anticipated purchasing at Sotheby's. Even though I was outbid, I decided to make the journey anyway, having other art business with Christie's and Sotheby's that needed attention. My interest in Jung's letters had grown over time, as they were the reading material of my weekly German tutorials. Together, my tutor and I would work on material from the two-volume set of *Collected Letters*, edited by Aniela Jaffé and Gerhard Adler. Over time, I found myself being drawn to those letters Jung wrote, in his later years, to regular people who would write for personal advice or the clarification of a dream or feeling. The singular kindness Jung showed toward these anonymous recipients touched me deeply. It occurred to me that, besides collecting them, perhaps I could do some scholarly work on them as well.

As I had really no idea how to proceed technically with such an idea, it seemed a natural next step to confer with someone who would, so I invited Sonu to lunch. I had heard of Sonu before, having read some of his articles and his excellent book, *Cult Fictions*. More importantly, I knew that he was editing Jung's *Red Book*, having seen the notification of that fact in the back of a recent newsletter of the International Association for Analytical Psychology. In fact, I still have that original announcement, which I keep with the advance copy of *The Red Book*, sent to me by Jim Mairs, the publisher at Norton. At the time, I thought it would be helpful for me to meet this fellow and ask his advice and help with my letters project as well as to talk to someone who was working on this magical volume.

In my life as a Jungian I had not been so lucky, having had the idea of its publication quickly and summarily squashed back in 1989 by Jung's son, Franz. At that time, while editor-in-chief of *Quadrant*, I had visited Franz to discuss Jung's interest in art in preparation for an issue entitled "Art and Soul." While at Seestrasse (Franz was most gracious and had invited me for tea), I took the risk of proposing a facsimile edition of *The Red Book* that might be published by Shambhala Press, which, at the time, was working closely with the Jung Foundation in New York and was publisher of *Quadrant*. My otherwise genial host turned quite aggressive and nearly shouted that "*The Red Book* would never be published!" adding, for extra measure, that I could not see the volume "because it was in a bank vault in Zürich, and that it would not be sold to a Texan who had offered him $5 million!" Seeing that I was startled at his outburst, Franz attempted to soothe me by showing me many other treasures, including a few of the now legendary black books. I spoke no more of *The Red Book*, but reveled in being permitted to handle what I now know to be its source material.

So, fourteen years later, I was now meeting Sonu for lunch to discuss, among other things, *The Red Book*. He chose a wonderful high-end Indian restaurant in the Mayfair section of London, called Benares. During our meal I asked about *The Red Book*, and Sonu told me that the funds required for the project's continuation were running critically low. I was astonished that the worldwide Jungian community had not been asked to contribute. It seemed inconceivable that such a project could run into financial problems, despite the fact that Sonu had, over time, spoken to many in the Jungian world about funding editorial work on *The Red Book* as well as on other unpublished material. As if turning away from further discussion about this, to my mind, improbable situation, we began speaking about the letters and how I envisioned my project. He asked me how many letters I thought Jung had written, perhaps to give me a sense of the parameters of my research. When I guessed 5,000, he shook his head and shared with me that tens of thousands of letters remained unpublished and virtually unknown in the Jung Archives at the Eidgenössische Technische Hochschule (ETH) in Zürich and elsewhere in the world, thousands of pages of unpublished seminar material and manuscript pages as well. In short, there was a lifetime's worth of scholarly work to do on the unpublished Jung.

I was stunned at the thought of all this treasure, for it was treasure to me, and I found myself overwhelmed and excited in a way that I had been only once or twice before in my life. Sonu kept his cool the whole time and, as I was about to hail a cab to take me to Christie's, I said to Sonu, "Why don't we start a foundation?" Right there on a street in Mayfair, July 4, 2003, at about 2:30 Greenwich Mean Time. I remember that he looked at me and said something like, "Sure, let's do that. Call me when you make headway." Driving away in the cab I knew that it wasn't a matter of headway, it was a matter of fate. I knew that a foundation, the Philemon Foundation, would come into existence and that my life had changed its course.

I didn't sleep that night, not one bit; I was inspired, seized by a daimon. I knew, or it knew, that once I got home, called a dear friend of mine, a self-taught Jungian layperson who loves Jung as I do, and explained the situation about *The Red Book* and the trove of unpublished material, the foundation would become a reality because he would help us fund its birth. And, after bursting into tears, so he did and here we are. Within a month after that, the three of us met and the plans for establishing the foundation were formalized. To commemorate our coming together as co-founders, Sonu created an anagram that used to be on our old website.

GF: What an extraordinary beginning. What happened next to you?

SM: Actually, something very strange but in keeping with the "given" nature of the project. By that I mean, of course I was captivated consciously by starting the foundation—it was incredibly exciting—but complementing that excitement were other sorts of experiences and synchronicities that seemed to be giving encouragement and help. One such repeated experience was what I have come to call "communion in the mudroom," that little area where we keep coats and boots and things just before leaving the backdoor of my house. On several occasions as I was passing through that space, I heard a voice in my head, quite audibly, instructing me to call people who might be able to help us. The voice told me to call you after twenty-four years of not being in any kind of contact, giving me the distinct feeling—no, *assuring* me—that you would be interested in this adventure and point out a new way to proceed. And of course you did, listening sympathetically and being enthused by the tale and putting me in touch with Nancy Furlotti and others who have helped. In that same mudroom, again the voice spoke to me and told me to call Jim Hollis, a dear friend and then the director of the Jung Center of Houston, to ask for help. It was he who facilitated Carolyn

Grant Fay's generosity, so much so that she became our patron and second major benefactor.

During this time as well, Sonu and I conferred frequently while I began seeking other potential donors. We both wanted to cast the net widely and to seek out friends of Jung who are not normally canvassed by Jungian organizations. We wanted the Philemon Foundation to be a grass-roots experience and to involve as many donors as possible. Our vision of the foundation's structure emerged intuitively. I think that Sonu, with his extensive academic and organizational experience, had a very good touch with this sort of thing. My strong suit was people; that is, having a feel for those who might be supporters of our work. And I began by simply telling the story as if it were a fairy tale because it really felt like it: "Did you know that there exists an incredible treasure trove of unpublished Jung that the world has never seen, that we need to see and can see, and that this historian, Sonu Shamdasani, and other scholars can make that invisible material visible? A treasure that is not hard to attain, perhaps?"

Simultaneously we were beginning to have conversations with Ulrich Hoerni, who was the director of the Erbengemeinschaft C.G. Jung, or the association of Jung's heirs, and now directs its nonprofit successor, the Stiftung der Werke von C.G. Jung or the Foundation for the Work of C.G. Jung. Pretty quickly the possibility of cooperation between our organizations began to crystallize. From these discussions came the agreement that is still the one with which we work at the present time. Thanks to his trust in Sonu, with whom he had been working for years on *The Red Book*, and a favorable impression of me, Ulrich Hoerni took the risk of joining with our vision.

GF: It is a remarkable story with so many moments and synchronicities without which the Philemon Foundation would not have come into being.

SM: Yes, it would seem that some sort of psychic critical mass had been reached. Sonu told me many stories about his attempts to do what we were able to do, but to no avail. There's no doubt about it, we were guided to it; I was guided to it. On every level it felt as if it were "given" to me, as if I were "called."

GF: Have you ever been called before?

SM: Once before did I feel called, some eighteen years ago when the world of decorative arts opened up to me. I fell passionately and completely in love with the work of the great British designer, Archibald Knox. From that call I went on to edit the definitive monograph on his life and work, to co-curate six exhibitions of his work in major museums, and to build the most lauded collection of his objects. Throughout that period of creative madness, despite nearly impoverishing my family and myself, I knew that I was in the service of a greater creativity than my own. I am proud to say that it was my effort that reestablished Knox as one of the greatest designers of the Art Nouveau and Arts and Crafts tradition.

But in terms of my life as a Jungian, this was another order of experience, this call. For the last thirty years of working as an analyst, even though I was one of three analysts who founded our local professional association, the Philadelphia Association of Jungian Analysts, in the early 1980s, as well as being a founding member of the Philadelphia Jung Seminar, our local training program, I would never have dreamed of anything on this level. Such professional activities were born out of a kind of extraverted necessity, if you will, but the Philemon Foundation, as it was to be thereafter named by Maggie Baron, was sheer inspiration; it was the call of something beyond my comprehension. You often said to me, when I was feeling overwhelmed or enormously stressed about the magnitude of the task, that I should "trust the process" because it was being guided by the Self. I'm sometimes a bit gun shy to make such judgments because they can sound so grand, but there's no doubt that this would never have come to fruition, enabling *The Red Book* to be published in the time that we could accomplish it, if it were not coming from some place other than me or my ego. As if to underscore this point, more than once I have felt Jung's presence in my life during this activity.

GF: Have you ever dreamt of Jung?

SM: Yes, I have. In one very memorable dream he simply appeared and said, "I am here with you." There are others, but this pretty much summed it up.

GF: In spite of all of this history, what I keep coming back to is the timing of it all, the "right moment" for it to happen despite all odds to the contrary. Isn't it true that some days before you went to London to meet Sonu on June 29th, you had a major car accident?

SM: That's right, it was terrifying. A taxicab and I collided on Park Avenue and 67th Street in New York City. I can't remember that much about the particular conditions of the accident except that before I knew it, I was in a trauma center on the Upper East Side. I was on an art-related errand when it happened. By all rights I should never have been going to London, let alone be alive. I saw the crash happening as if in slow motion. I hit the brakes and figured, "This is it," but then the airbags deployed and it was all over, just like that. In the end I was burned by the airbags but was relatively uninjured, miraculously, with the exception of some whiplash, sore muscles, and a shaken spirit. Thankfully, no one else was hurt. But this did not stop me from going to London, because I felt compelled to do so.

Ultimately, yet another synchronicity was involved. It did not escape my notice that the accident happened on the same block as the 67th Street Armory in New York City—that very place where I discovered my passion for the decorative arts. In that Armory, every year for years a major antique show would occur in November, and it was there, at one of these shows in the early 1990s, that I discovered Knox. After the accident I reflected from a soul perspective that at that very moment, in one shattering moment, one daimon gave way to another; it was as if a part of my soul was wrenched from the decorative arts and found its way back to me in a completely different incarnation five days later in London. Some kind of transfiguration occurred, and my world shifted. It was as if I had been reborn.

GF: Do you think that your being an analyst and Sonu being a historian must have been just the right combination as a team to start the foundation?

SM: Unquestionably. First and foremost, nothing would have happened without Sonu's impeccable credentials as a scholar, and in particular, as a Jung scholar. No enterprise of this sort would ever have been possible without Sonu and his gifts. As for the other side of the equation, how to reach the broader Jungian world to solicit help, being an analyst was critical on several levels. Most obviously, the fact that I have been involved with Jungian psychology since I was eighteen and a practicing analyst for thirty years created a basis for my familiarity with and love for the material itself. I mean that in both an intellectual and a feeling way. Jung and his work are living realities for me, and it was not hard to become the person to elicit that feeling in others and to encourage their participation as supporters of the project. And by eliciting support, I mean also asking for money. I had no compunction about doing so because our mission was so absolutely right, and I could convey that sense of rightness with enthusiasm and utter conviction.

It also helped a great deal that I began my training in the early 1970s in Zürich, when many of Jung's students were still alive and teaching, including my beloved analyst, Liliane Frey, and when many who are in leadership roles in the various Jungian professional groups were training. Being a fellow analyst, and one with deep connections to the history of our discipline and to its Zurich birthplace, created, I think, a kind of felt trustworthiness so that when I reached out to talk about our foundation, I was given an ear.

Throughout my time as an analyst, I have had a passion for the historical side of Jung, even before meeting Sonu. As I mentioned, already in the 1980s I was deeply interested in the issue of Jung and anti-Semitism. And finally, being a collector of Jung's work, I had a firsthand appreciation and love for the physical material, which took a quantum leap when we started the foundation. To me, it is the greatest treasure that there is, and as an inveterate treasure hunter, the Philemon Foundation allowed me to really delve into this wonderful material and to see what can only be described as magical things.

GF: Can you say more about your work as an editor and an author?

SM: Certainly. My editorship at *Quadrant* was an extremely important learning experience that had a direct impact on the establishment of the Philemon Foundation. At first, I was quite hesitant to take on *Quadrant*—in fact, I turned it down two times—but Aryeh Maidenbaum, who was then the Executive Director of the Jung Foundation in New York City, wouldn't take no for an answer. Because I understood myself well enough to know that I was not principally a scholar or a theoretician, and when I compared myself to the editors of the other Jungian journals at the time, I wondered what I could bring to *Quadrant* to make it unique.

During this period James Hillman was editor of *Spring*, John Beebe was at the helm of the *San Francisco Library Journal*, and Ernst Rossi was editing your journal, *Psychological Perspectives*. These are men, to me, of great intellect, and given my trepidations about not being principally a scholar, or a thinking type, it was critical for me to figure out what my voice or role would be in the Jungian world. Very quickly, the realization came to me that I'm a connector, a feeling type who can see and value the work of others and who could take delight in making it possible for that work to be showcased and to be brought forward into the world. I realized very quickly that my gift, and my joy, is to enable the gifts of others to be seen and shared. An additional realization was that *Quadrant* could also become a place where I could not only bring together talented people but also create a publication where deeply interesting material could be presented in an elegant, artistically compelling form—a task that called on my first love, what I left behind to enter the world of Jungian psychology, that of being an artist. In the early 1970s, I went to Zürich with every intention of being a painter, but as is the case with so many of us, I followed a different path.

Quadrant allowed me to be that artist, and I refined that role with my work in the decorative arts when I showcased the work of Archibald Knox. Not only did I edit the books about him, I co-designed them as well as helping to plan the exhibitions I co-curated. Beauty of presentation was for me as critical an expression of the soul as the information a publication could convey. I like to think that I have brought that sensibility to the graphic presentation of the Philemon Foundation. And so it was with the Philemon Foundation. I could see instantly that my job was to support Sonu's scholarship and to bring others together who could support our mission, including other scholars, donors, and friends of Jung.

Being an analyst and having this kind of spirit was just the right combination. Being familiar with the Jungian world, having the pedigree of being "Zürich-born," and having a personal connection with so many in this world (even though I had deliberately avoided the political side of our Jungian organizations) gave me a wide range. I was able to reach out ecumenically to convince disparate and, at times, conflicting groups and individuals to join our work. Sonu provided the depth of scholarship that would do justice to Jung's genius, as well as the solid, organizational knowledge, and I was the net that harvested the souls who would join us.

GF: You know, often we think about spirit as air or wind, or something of an active nature that can make a fire much larger. I think that the spirit you brought to this must have been like blowing on a hot coal and adding fuel to it, because you bring tremendous spirit. There's no question about it.

SM: I was on fire, and I think that Sonu and I had an extraordinary synergy. We saw things very clearly and very much in the same way in terms of purpose and strategy. From the start we decided to take the high road about creating the foundation and not get embroiled in power struggles that were bound to happen. And despite the people who were doubtful, if not openly resistant, sometimes most unpleasantly, we would soldier on.

GF: Did you have many disappointments when you were looking for fundraising among colleagues?

SF: Some, but I would say that on the whole we were supported by a number of analysts and that number has been on the increase over the last year or two. What is more important, however, is that thousands of *Red Books* are being sold, and our endeavor is a huge success.

GF: How has the funding for *The Red Book* been accomplished?

SM: It was really quite simple but hard work nonetheless. We reached out to those who love Jung's work and caught the interest of individuals and institutions alike. Donations have been as small as the $5 bill that came wrapped in newspaper in an envelope addressed in a clearly elderly, infirm hand and as large as seven figures.

GF: And the Philemon Foundation probably receives money from the sale of *The Red Book*?

SM: No, we receive no royalties whatsoever from its sale. We receive no royalties whatsoever from any book that we fund.

GF: Where do the royalties go?

SF: They reside with the Stiftung der Werke von C.G. Jung, which is the foundation for the literary estate of C.G. Jung. The funds do not go to the Jung family but to supporting the literary estate itself.

GF: The foundation seems to be going along in a very good way. What do you think happened to you in the process of creating the Philemon Foundation?

SM: That's an interesting question, Gilda, and I am not sure I can be very clear, because whatever happened is still happening, so I can only make some preliminary observations. In a certain sense, being given the opportunity to establish the Philemon Foundation fulfills a part of my destiny as a devoted Jungian. I discovered Jung when I was eighteen years old and have been, for nearly forty years, just like what was reported in the *New York Times* article about *The Red Book*, religiously devoted to Jung and his work. To set the story straight, though, when my daughter, who was at the time in fifth grade or so, asked "what religion" I was, as part of a homework assignment to interview her mom and dad about our backgrounds, and I answered "Jungian," I in no way meant that Jung or Jungian thought was a religion. What I meant was that this path I have been following for so many years is just this one, and I do so "religiously" with all the challenges of any worldview or life system. With all of this in mind, I delight in the notion that I was the catalyst who got the Philemon Foundation going, because my entire Jungian journey has been improbable, and wonderfully so. It strikes me that if you look at where I come from, you would never have thought that someone like me would have played such a role in this important endeavor.

GF: When you say, "where you come from," do you mean in terms of your family or your socioeconomic background?

SM: Both—from a lower-middle-class *shtetl*-like Jewish experience, born in Brooklyn, raised in the backwoods of Queens, New York City.

GF: And you think a parson's son had a better opportunity than you to become what Jung became?

SM: Point well taken! Of course you're right, and it's probably so for many of us who love Jung's work. What has all of this done to me? I feel honored, I feel humbled, and I feel that a part of me has been completed. It's given me the opportunity to pay back the gift of life that Jung's work has provided, that I was lucky enough to discover through Liliane Frey. She is the guardian angel of this entire adventure.

GF: She was your analyst?

SM: Yes, she was my analyst and became my dear friend. I spent the ten years after my departure from Zürich visiting her often, sometimes three times a year. She had great faith in me, and I am grateful to her. To some extent, my work for the Philemon Foundation is also dedicated to her.

GF: I understand this.

SM: I also think that I've matured along the way, learning how complex organizations are and a lot about how to manage forces in the world that are far larger than I. And, I must say, I have come face to face, despite being inspired, with the limits of what I can and cannot do. At the end of the day, I am not an organizational person, and I greatly respect those who are. But most of all, I have learned, yet again, that if something moves me, if I am seized like I was, then I must become the dedicated servant.

GF: And what has it cost?

SM: A great deal, actually. For the last six years I have had two full-time jobs, directing the Philemon Foundation and practicing as an analyst. I also have a family with kids in college and one coming up to college. I have worked at least 70 to 80 hours per week for all of this time on my various jobs.

GF: You must have a very understanding wife?

SM: I do have a very understanding wife, but every now and then you have to pay back. When I don't have family responsibilities, my weekends are almost always consumed with Philemon work.

GF: This leads me to the next question. In December 2009 you stepped down as president of the Philemon Foundation. What prompted that decision, especially now at this moment when *The Red Book* has been published? And what do you think about the future of the Philemon Foundation?

SM: I stepped down from the presidency and my administrative role as well because I have the strong discernment that I have accomplished what I set out to accomplish—to establish a foundation to support Sonu and the other scholars who are getting the unpublished work of Jung into publication, and most specifically, *The Red Book*. That wonderful event has taken place, and we have a healthy donor base of over one thousand people. My job is done. It has been a visionary job that reflects the visionary component in my character that I have described as being seized by a daimon and being compelled to live out its demands. I knew instinctively that the watershed moment for me was going to be the publication of *The Red Book*. I sensed that when this occurred, an energy shift would also happen—and it has. For the foundation, the visionary period is giving way to a time of consolidation and expansion. We have a good team in the Philemon Foundation board, and our new co-presidents, Nancy Furlotti and Judith Harris, along with Sonu and other colleagues, will steer Philemon into its mature phase.

What do I think about its future? When I imagine it, I see a wide and long horizon of project after project coming to fruition, of volumes of letters, manuscripts, seminars, and perhaps even someday, the original protocols that were the basis of *Memories, Dreams, Reflections* coming into print. I see a blossoming collaboration among the various Jungian families and factions conjoining with the Philemon Foundation as the locus of moving Jung, Jung scholarship, and Jungian wisdom into the next century. I see the Philemon Foundation as being the pulsing heart of a vast, newly energized body of friends who are vitally interested in Jung and his great work.

GF: What role will you have?

SM: I will stay on the board and do what I can to further our mission, and I will enjoy my designation as President Emeritus.

GF: How has reading *The Red Book* affected you personally, apart from having been, like the producer of a movie, so involved in its publication?

SM: Let me tell you a story. I was asked by a group of retired people from a local church to lead a group on Jung. The group has been in existence for a while and has had some very good theoretical instruction on Jung from other analysts. Instead of doing more theory, I asked them to read the fabulous chapter in Memories called "Confrontation with the Unconscious," which I've read many, many times. Reading it in preparation for our first meeting, which was last Thursday, I was stunned at how the material felt after having read *The Red Book*. It was as if I were looking through this chapter into something deeper. An entirely new way of seeing had been opened to me, as if I were looking into the depths of Jung's soul. I understood viscerally now, as Sonu has often said, that Jung wrote in code, that interwoven through so much of his post-*Red Book* writings are intimations of, if not direct references to, what is contained in *The Red Book*. Although my understanding of *The Red Book* is just beginning, having read it a couple of times, it feels like a constant companion, a spiritual, psychological, and emotional companion that changes my relationship to Jung simply by existing. Consequently it inspires my own inner work; it gives the feeling that the layers of depth within me, by knowing more about the layers of depth within Jung, are coming to life. The *Red Book* is an enormous encouragement to my process of individuation.

GF: That's a beautiful way of putting it, Steve. Finally, what impact can *The Red Book* have on readers at large, do you think?

SM: Gilda, the best way to answer this question is to circle back to the conditions that led to the birth of the Philemon Foundation in the first place: my captivation by Jung's incredible compassion for the common person. It all arose from experiencing Jung's availability to letter writers who sought counsel from this great man. Seeing myself as part of that tribe of commoners, I have made it my goal in my analytical work to mediate the complexities of Jung's work to "regular people." I feel deeply that it is my destiny to help make Jung's work and wisdom accessible to those who would otherwise have limited access. Thus it is extremely exciting to sit with a group of retired people, with little real exposure to how Jung's work actually affects life, and have them be drawn into the incredible richness and possibility that is their own inner lives.

GF: Since Jung was the kind of person who liked regular people, as you call them, and could speak to gardeners and farmers and so forth, and really kept that side of himself very much alive, I think that this would make a great deal of sense to him. From the beginning of his career Jung struggled with the professional world, wanting, on the one hand, to be part of it, but understanding, on the other, that those professions often missed the point. Even now, I know people who have never been in a Jung institute but who have read the *Collected Works*; regular people, they just read the *Collected Works* and thought them brilliant.

SM: To that point, Gilda, my friend—that third person who helped us start the Philemon Foundation—is just such a regular person. He deserves our gratitude for his willingness to initially fund us. He's a self-taught individual, not even college educated, who came to Jung in his forties and lives Jung's insights deeply. He is the archetypal "regular" person. His kind of deep natural love of the psyche and of Jung's work and genius is, for me, at the very core of this great adventure.

Chapter 8

FELLINI SATYRICON

Originally published in *Psychological Perspectives*[73]

... what is reality?
—F. Fellini

... what is an interview?
—G. Frantz

The theater lights went on and still I sat in my seat not wanting to leave. The people who had shared my experience also sat waiting. Finally, one by one, we rose and left the theater. As I reached the street I hesitated briefly, wondering if I should go back and see Fellini Satyricon *a second time. Later, another time, I thought, but not right now. Now I only wanted to talk to someone about this extraordinary film. I wanted to talk with Fellini himself, and that was how this unique experience came about. I decided to go and see him and talk to him about what I felt was the cinematic masterpiece of our time. The airports, planes, arrangements—all this seemed unimportant to me, it was Fellini who was important.*

The taxi drove up a long path to the house that was on a hill overlooking Rome. It was a private looking house, somewhat mysterious. The architecture was very old and elegant. I paid the driver and rang the doorbell. Mrs. Fellini, the actress Guilietta Masina, asked me to enter. All smiles and charm, she took me down a long marble corridor,

73 Gilda Frantz, "Fellini Satyricon," *Psychological Perspectives* 1(2), (1970): 157-161.

through a study and into a garden terrace where her husband was sitting having coffee. He waved me to a seat and we began the interview.

FRANTZ: I have heard so many conflicting reports about what people "think" *Satyricon* is about that I feel a need to clarify that. One friend said it was about the pre-Christian era in Rome and that one could understand by seeing the film why Christ appeared when he did. That is to say, how desparately he was needed. Another saw it as a homosexual picture about two young lovers who seek adventure together; that the theme is entirely about homosexual love. Still another described it to me as un-understandable. You must understand that these comments were all made by intelligent people whose opinions I value, and yet I saw the film and agree with none of these points of view. How do you explain this?

FELLINI: I don't. That is what makes art and creativity so exciting and why it is that I continue to work in the medium of the moving picture. Hopefully what I accomplish when I complete a film is three-fold. I can say that I have grown inwardly having developed and completed a germ of an intuition; someone might be touched by it or changed by it, or feel something new and disturbing in his otherwise complacent life, so that even though he did not see the same thing I did, he at least saw; and finally, if it is true that I am un-understandable, at the very least the viewer will become angry because he did not understand and that is not nothing. I have never hoped that anyone would see precisely what I did in any film I ever made. Some have, of course, but that is not my goal.

FRANTZ: What gave you the idea to make *Satyricon*? Why did you choose that particular story? It seemed somewhat flimsy to me.

FELLINI: One night I had a dream. I awoke in the middle of the night and could not go back to sleep, so I got up and wrote it down. Later that morning I could not shake the mood of the dream. You understand this? I walked to my office and still I thought about this dream. Late into the evening it was still coming into my consciousness in short flashes. I began to write down some of these inner impressions, just a line here, a word there, and soon I had a few pages of what I thought my dream was saying to me. Out of this dream came the movie. As to why I chose *Satyricon*, I would say it was a convenient hook upon which I could hang my images, my ideas. You do not throw your coat upon the floor, eh? An artist needs something also on which to hang his creative thought . . . one does not use thin air. I used this particular story because it enabled me to depict all that my dream said to me in a way that was challenging, enlightening, and artistic.

FRANTZ: Will you tell us the dream?

FELLINI: No. The artist's only responsibility to his public is to interpret what is in his unconscious, to know what has universal content and meaning, not necessarily to reveal the *entire* contents of his unconscious. I will not tell my actual dream, but you see I have shared the results with the world! My dreams are very real to me and I listen to them very closely. Have you never noticed how cinematic the language of dreams is? The way people move in a dream, for instance. That fascinates me . . . they very often just appear without rhyme or reason, but they are needed and they come. I often have people who walk through the backgrounds of my films in just that way to complete and balance a scene. I see each scene as a painting and the characters in the back are terribly important, each extra, each figure, terribly important. They are not *just* background, anymore than a shadowy figure in a dream is background.

FRANTZ: In your opening scene the young hero, Encolpius, stands in front of a wall that is scarred with the graffiti of centuries. The sky seems sullen and oppressive as we watch the fair hero lamenting the loss of his young lover, Giton, whom his best friend, Ascyltus has sold as a slave. What were you trying to say?

FELLINI: What did I say to *you* in that scene? What I think is of little importance now. What matters is, did it speak to you and what did it say?

FRANTZ: It said that man always leaves his mark wherever he goes, and he has done so since the very beginning of time. He began with cave paintings and has progressed to leaving marks on trees, walls, and toilets. Not just his name, but his message. It also said to me that the wall separates man and his spirit and the two must be reunited. The wall seemed to say that man does not change, only times change. I had a similar impression when I saw the opening scene of *8½*, of man's unchanging, unutterable isolation and helplessness in the confrontation with his own nature. That is what spoke to me in *Satyricon*.

FELLINI: I have always contended that my films are about real people and reality. My dreams are my reality. I have been accused of peopling my films with unbelievable faces and bodies; blue-faced women, sideshow monstrosities; of being gory and erotic and debauched. The unconscious is amoral. It is unjudging. Anything can enter one's unconscious, and it usually does, the results either terrifying or tantalizing the dreamer. I try in my film to be loyal to that in my own unconscious which is debauched, erotic, yes even gory. Do you remember the scene in which the slave's hand is sacrificed? I have seen worse in my dreams. That was only a distillation.

FRANTZ: I think my favorite character in *Satyricon* was the poet, although Encolpius was very handsome and sympathetic. Yet I felt the poet was the most important character because it was he who tried to help Encolpius regain his lost potency, his manhood, and it was he who knew that Encolpius should see the sorceress who had been bewitched by a wizard. It was in her fiery passage that he was reborn. Also, when the poet is dead, it is then that Encolpius begins his journey to Africa, alone this time, having been through his own "Inferno" of transformation.

FELLINI: I, too, liked the poet. The poet represented the archetype of the old wise man who befriends the youth and guides him, almost imperceptably, through the nightmare called *life*.

FRANTZ: I read in *Time* magazine that you were considered a Jungian moviemaker, and that *Satyricon* is considered the first really Jungian movie. What do you say to that?

FELLINI: I laugh loudly! To me it implies that I use the archetypes in a mythical way, perhaps the way Jung would have if he had been a moviemaker instead of a psychologist. I listen to the language of the unconscious, I interpret it, reshape it, color it and make it move and speak and reach down into other viewers' unconsciouses. Jung was a very contemporary man, and I feel myself trying to speak to contemporary creative problems. My films are my attempts to solve some of the problems which we, in our time, are faced with and to attempt to understand them. I was very flattered when *Time* wrote that, very flattered, but I feel that others who make films are trying to do what I try to do.

FRANTZ: Do you consider yourself a Jungian?

FELLINI: Yes and no. I had an advisor on my film who knows a great deal about the way Jung understood symbolism. That was very helpful. But I am an artist and my first responsibility is to myself. I consider myself a man who learns from everyone and everything. What has changed in me that *Time* did not call *8½* a Jungian movie? I would say that I *am* a Jungian, but an artist first.

FRANTZ: Some portions of *Satyricon* fascinated me, but admittedly I was confused. Encolpius's marriage to the one-eyed warrior during the voyage of the slave ship was exciting in terms of drama and imagination, but I really didn't understand.

FELLINI: What is so wrong with not knowing, with confusion? What is wrong with not knowing all of the time? Do you always understand everything you read? Let it puzzle you, gnaw at you, then you will have the joy of discovery when it finally does become meaningful.

FRANTZ: It *is* puzzling me and gnawing at me and I am trying. I hope I will be loyal to the quest of understanding, Mr. Fellini, as you have been courageous in exploring your creative imagination. I can tell that I have taken up too much of your time and that it is the moment to say goodbye. I am so very grateful for this visit.

FELLINI: It was my pleasure. *Buon qiorno.*

Walking down the path leading away from Fellini's house, I could feel the rustle of the autumn leaves under my feet. ". . . what I think is of little importance now." Is that what he said? Did I really sit talking with him on his terrace overlooking the ancient city of Rome? Or did I imagine it all?

Chapter 9

SHAME

Originally presented at the Tenth International Congress of
Analytical Psychology[74]

In the film, *Oh, God!* God is on earth as an "ordinary" person. At one
point God, played by George Burns, says, "I made two mistakes when
I created the world. The first mistake was inventing shame, and the
second was that I made the avocado pit too big!" The avocado pit is an
image for the seed that gives us the potential of becoming. It is the core
of the ego-ideal–shadow–Self axis. Like the avocado pit, shame/shadow
takes up a great deal of room.

From the moment I read the title of Hultberg's talk, I felt a deep
sense of what it means to have shame stand between the idealized ego
and the Self. While his paper touches upon many aspects of shame psychologically, socially, and anthropologically, I will focus on shame as
related to individuation. Thus I will elaborate on the theme rather than
offer a critique of his paper.

One of Hultberg's examples that particularly caught my interest is
that of the 76-year-old woman who found herself suffering from an
inoperable tumor. This story has certain parallels within our own Jungian community. We too practice a philosophy. Being exposed on a daily
basis to the radiating effects of the unconscious is inflating. As recep-
tors of the powerful archetypal energies of the transference, we analysts
are prone to godlike projections and to hubris. Many of us are directed

---

74 Gilda Frantz, "Shame" (paper presented at the Tenth International Congress of
Analytical Psychology, Berlin, Germany, September 2-9, 1986).

by our own individuation process, yet like Hultberg's patient, we may have a misconception about the rewards of individuation. Do we have the notion that we will not have to suffer the humiliation and shame of a painful illness or death if we pay attention to our dreams and active imagination? Here I refer particularly to cancer, which seems to be the most stigmatized disease for those of us in the healing arts. Ironically, individuals who deal with pain and suffering often seem to have painful deaths or illnesses themselves. The notion that inner development can make one immune to such a fate is, indeed, a form of hubris.

Careful attention to one's dreams can guarantee the rewards of consciousness but not a so-called "good death." The idea that we will be saved from the shame of illness or suffering if we listen to the unconscious is something we might pass on, unconsciously, to our analysands, as though the unconscious were a benign and good god. Yet nothing could be further from the truth. While one needs to prepare for death by understanding one's own myth and by having a religious attitude toward the mysterious and wondrous experience of life itself, nothing can ensure that we will die gloriously, or even painlessly. If there is such a thing as a good death, it is a conscious death, one without shame. Consciousness does not prevent pain or suffering; it can only help prevent meaningless suffering.

Shame belongs in the same category as terror and anxiety. Natural creatures, that is, unconscious ones, are spared such troubles. The consequence of shame is that it pulls one out of containment in nature; that is what happened to Hultberg's cancer patient. In spite of her spiritual practices, she developed a serious illness and felt that she would be deprived of her idealized image of death—that she should die while meditating and be sent to a higher incarnation.

The issue of shame belongs to human consciousness. The fairy tale of the ugly duckling is an illustration. It is only when the "ugly duckling" becomes aware of his true identity that he ceases to feel ashamed of his appearance. His consciousness is expanded to fit his true Self. This is what Jung called the development of personality. The hardest task each of us has in life is to become aware of our higher personality. An important point Hultberg makes is that feeling shame produces the wish that the earth would open under our feet and swallow us. Being swallowed is the return to the mother, the desire to return to the womb, a hiding place of dark safety. It also signals the death of an ego-ideal. This ego consciousness has to die—be swallowed—in order for a new awareness of oneself to expand and include the shadow or the dark side of the Self. The danger of being swallowed is the loss of one's consciousness. If shame is to be understood as accompanying an experience of the Self, then being swallowed is the desire to re-enter paradise and return to an unconscious state—to slip away from the consciousness of one's own dark shadow.

Jungian analytic practices are of a spiritual nature; they involve *spiritus* and *materia*, soul and body. We all have our analytic secrets about which we might feel shame if exposed. An example of such a case was presented by the late Kieffer Frantz. A female analysand was having difuculties in her analysis with him. He suggested that she consult another therapist in our Los Angeles Jungian community to discuss these difficulties. The patient asked, "Wouldn't you rather I go to a therapist outside of your own community?" She implied that there would be shame involved for him if their analytic relationship were exposed; she said she was trying to protect his reputation.

This was not a concretized relationship, nor was there any physical contact. Their analytic relationship contained a great deal of heat nonetheless. This is a good example of the analyst's not trying to hide from exposure, of being in relationship to both ego-ideal and Self. One of the definitions of shame has to do with being unclothed or exposed. Similarly, one of the definitions of the word *bereft* is to be naked, to have one's clothes taken away.

Shame is the gristle we must chew on in order to integrate our shadow complex. For some it is totally indigestible. In my own practice I worked with a woman who carried a tremendous amount of guilt and shame from an early trauma: witnessing something within her family that was shameful to her. She dreamed of being back in the old neighborhood and having something unchewable in her mouth, and she couldn't find a place to spit it out. She simply wasn't able to swallow it. Finally she spit it into a public drinking fountain with a great sense of relief. The shadow complex could not be integrated in a personal sense but needed a more collective container.

Shame has to do with individuation because it results from a conflict between the ego-ideal and the shadow and is thereby related to the Self. Shame as an integral part of individuation is well illustrated by the story of Genesis, and in particular by "The Fall." In the beginning there was chaos, then creation, and then Yahweh created Adam and Eve. He placed them in the Garden, provided them with all the good things of life, and warned them not to eat of the fruit of either the Tree of the Knowledge of good and evil or the Tree of Life, for death would surely follow their transgression. There is breathtaking abundance; this is Paradise. The two walk hand in hand, bodies touching at the hips, flesh to flesh. Their bareness is pleasant, unnoticed, neither cared about nor thought about. "Now both of them were naked, the man and his wife, but they felt no shame in front of each other."[75]

The serpent seduced Eve into tasting the fruit of the Tree of the Knowledge of good and evil, telling her that she would not die but rather would be like God in all respects. She, in turn, seduced Adam into eating the fruit, and then Yahweh appeared. When He approached, Adam and Eve saw that they were naked and felt shame and covered themselves. Yahweh knew by their shame that they had transgressed and disobeyed Him. He then cursed the serpent, Adam, and Eve individually; aware that they would now be tempted to eat of the Tree of Life and become immortal, He cast them out of Paradise. Yahweh saw that Adam and Eve felt shame. It was the capacity to feel shame that told Yahweh that they were now conscious, for shame occurs only where there is consciousness, and consciousness involves the shadow. Their shame focused on their nakedness because the body is container of the soul, and the soul coexists with the shadow. The body contains the seed and the egg from which life has its source.

The myth of Genesis involves the eternal problem of containing the opposites, Yahweh and the serpent, within each of us. Each of us carries opposing energies, first urging us toward further growth and then warning us of the consequences if we listen. If we do not listen, we avoid

---

75 Genesis 2:25, *Jerusalem Bible*.

shame but we remain unconscious. If we do listen, we lose our attachment to the ego-ideal, our innocence, and try to cover ourselves and hide. Shame is the price we pay for becoming increasingly conscious human beings.

Part 3

NATURE

Personality is the supreme realization of the innate idiosyncrasy of a living being. It is an act of high courage flung in the face of life, the absolute affirmation of all that constitutes the individual, the most successful adaptation to the universal conditions of existence coupled with the greatest possible freedom for self-determination.

—C.G. Jung[76]

---

76 C.C. Jung, "The Development of Personality," CW 17, ¶ 289.

Chapter 10

CARRYING THE OPPOSITES WITHIN ONESELF

A Book Review

Originally published in *San Francisco Jung Journal* [77]

As I contemplate reviewing yet another book on "the nature of homo-sexuality," my thoughts focus on the eruption of the cultural shadow that occurred a year ago in Laramie, Wyoming. I refer to the horrific torture and murder of Matthew Shephard, small in stature but (as his uncle described him) "large of heart and soul." What can anyone say to a culture in which a gay, twenty-one-year-old is savagely beaten and left to die tied to a fence in a small town in Wyoming?

Matthew Shephard is not an isolated case of gay bashing. Such events are on the increase in America today. There have been many murders of gay men and lesbian women that did not manage to capture the com-passion of the entire nation, as did Matthew's. It would seem that being homosexual is still punishable by death in many parts of our country, and that despite much cultural interest in the possibilities of diversity, being different is frequently perceived as an insult to the rest of society. I have interviewed a number of gay men about their early childhood, and most of them have told me of a painful feeling, even then, that they were "different," "didn't fit in," and had "no place to hide." In Japan there is a saying that the nail that sticks up gets hammered down. Something was

---

77 Gilda Frantz, "Carrying the Opposites within Oneself: A Book Review," *The San Francisco Jung Institute Library Journal*, 18(2), (1999): 9-19.

visible that caused these gay children the pain and humiliation of having to be hammered down.

In his timely and beautifully written *Changing Ones*, Will Roscoe attempts to discover what this difference might be, taking a historical approach to the way it has been addressed on the American continent by native and by colonizing cultures. He writes that in the mid-sixteenth century, when Vasco Núñez de Balboa encountered forty *pathicos foeminol amictu* (male homosexuals dressed as women) in Panama, he had them put to the dogs. The scene is illustrated in sadomasochistic detail in Théodore de Bry's *Collectiones Peregrinationum*. "A fine action of an honourable and Catholic Spaniard, commented one historian a hundred years after."[78] The explorers who came after Balboa also took note of Native American men who were different from the other men of the tribe. They saw that some of them wore women's clothing and did women's work, and that some cohabited with other men, living as "husband" and "wife." To the explorers' puzzlement, these men had found a place of respect in the tribal community. A glaring difference between the situation for these "feminine" homosexual men then and now is that the tribe to which the berdache (two-spirit) men belonged supported their right to be different, and in fact felt its own sense of specialness to be blessed by men and women who could add to its reservoir of genders.

Roscoe presents a solid case that beside traditional masculinity and femininity, there are two more genders to consider. Although this is not a new idea, it is such a powerful concept one wonders that it has taken so long to be articulated this well. The notion of multiple genders that Roscoe derives from his study of Native American culture gives another dimension to the place of gay men and lesbian women in our present-day society. In Roscoe's thorough glossary he cites tribes, tribal names for males and females of the other two genders, and the source of his research. It is interesting to note that although some tribes had only one name for these "others," like the inadequate present-day *homosexual*, the Navajo had many names for men and women it considered to belong to the third and fourth genders. (The "third gender" refers to male and sometimes female berdaches; the "fourth gender" refers exclusively to

78 Will Roscoe, *Changing Ones: Third and Fourth Genders in Native North America*, 4.

female berdaches.) The Navajo names are *nutlys, nadtli, nu'tle, nadle, nadleeh, nadleehi*. None refer to sexuality as such. Rather, they mean "he changes," "being transformed," "that which changes," "one who changes time and again." The image of transformation from one way of being to another reminded me about my own experience raising a gay child. My son seemed to be like all other children until he was around three years old, and then "he changed." I will say more about this a little later on.

Roscoe supports his careful research with many tables, glossaries, and photographs. His chapter notes are very helpful. He lists the many names of gay men and lesbian women given them by various tribes such as the Inuit, Arapaho, Blackfoot, Cheyenne, Cree, Ojibwa, Apache, Chumash, Zuni, Hopi, Mohave, and Dakota to name only a small portion of his list. Each tribe had unique names, some of which are translated to mean, more or less, berdache. Others have a different slant, such as *woman pretenders, man pretenders; manly-hearted woman; man transformed into a woman*; and *boy whose sex changes at birth*. There are amazing illustrations from archival material of men and women who were "different": Roscoe has scoured letters, government sources, and every kind of material that might bring light to this subject. The following is an example:

> The physician Holder wrote what may be the earliest description of Osh-tisch. "One of the *boté* of my acquaintance is a splendidly formed fellow," he wrote in 1889, "of prepossessing face, in perfect health, active in movement, and happy in disposition. . . . He is five feet eight inches high, weighs one hundred and fifty-eight pounds, and has a frank, intelligent face—being an Indian, of course, beardless. He is thirty-three years of age and has worn woman's dress for twenty-eight years." Holder offered the *boté* money to undergo a medical examination, and true to nineteenth century faith in biological determinism, he inspected his genitals to determine whether they were "in position and shape altogether normal." (They were.) According to Holder, this *boté* had lived for two years with a well-known male Indian. "It is not, however, the usual habit of the *boté* to form a 'partnership' with a single man. He is, like the female members of this tribe, ready to

accommodate any male desiring his services." The preferred sexual practice of *boté*, Holder reported, was to perform fellatio on men. [Little had changed sixty years later, Roscoe writes, when Ford and Beach reported that four *boté* in the tribe were regularly visited by young men for oral sex.][79]

Roscoe recounts that Osh-tisch joined forces with General George Crook to fight in the Battle of the Rosebud. I had never heard of this battle, but a historian quoted by Roscoe tells us "it involved more troops, had fewer casualties, lasted for most of a day and was of far greater historical significance" than Custer's last stand.[80] Roscoe has another story from this battle:

> A young woman named Pretty-shield had watched the Crow warriors leave her village to join [General] Crook. Fifty years later, she recalled their adventures for the journalist Frank Linderman:
>
> "Did the men ever tell you anything about a woman who fought with Three-stars on the Rosebud?"
>
> "No," I replied, wondering.
>
> "Ahh, they do not like to tell of it," she chuckled. "But I will tell you about it. We Crows all know about it. I shall not be stealing anything from the men by telling the truth."
>
> "Yes, a Crow woman fought with Three-stars on the Rosebud, two of them did, for that matter; but one of them was neither a man nor a woman. She looked like a man, and yet she wore woman's clothing, and she had the heart of a woman. Besides, she did a woman's work. Her name was Finds-them-and-kills-them. She was not a man, and yet not a woman," Pretty-shield repeated. "She was not as strong as a man, and yet she was wiser than a woman," she said, musingly, her voice scarcely audible.
>
> "The other woman," she went on, "was a wild one who had no man of her own. She was both bad and brave this one. Her name was The-other-magpie; and she was pretty.[81]

79 Roscoe, *Changing Ones*, 30.
80 Roscoe, *Changing Ones*, 30.
81 Frank B. Linderman, quoted in Roscoe, *Changing Ones*, 31-33.

As the narrative continued, the woman called Pretty-shield told how these women . . .

> brought glory to the Crows by their brave deeds that day. When a warrior named Bull Snake was wounded by a Lakota and fell from his horse, Finds-them-and-kills-them "dashed up to him, got down from her horse, and stood over him, shooting at the [Lakota] as rapidly as she could load her gun and fire."

Both of these women were honored.

Native American people have been subject to repeated genocide, first by explorers from Spain and France, then by our Pilgrim forefathers and foremothers and the diseases they carried from the Old World, by the avarice of the pioneering movement West, and finally by being robbed of the natural support of their tribal lands. These unique people, who have not quite vanished from the face of the earth, understood and accepted gender diversity. They exhibited their empathy by making a place of honor within their tribal systems for those men and women who were distinguished by non-ordinary gender characteristics. The parents of a man or woman the foreign conquerors named *berdache* considered themselves blessed to have such a special offspring, and such families were honored by the tribe for their contribution to the life of the tribe. Berdaches were not ostracized or segregated in any way from the life of the tribe.

Having raised a gay son, I have given a lot of thought to this part of Roscoe's book. What a difference it would have made if the culture within which our family lived in the 1950s and 1960s had had the legacy of thinking of "different" children as gifted and valuable to the community. What many gay children experience instead is isolation, humiliation, and pain in growing up. Not infrequently they experience rejection both by family and society. I am convinced that when parents and society begin to understand how wonderfully unique their gay sons and daughters are, we will all benefit. Today there are quite a few young parents who are making an effort to understand their gay children and not reject them for being different, but this enlightened minority is not enough to shift society's prevailing attitude toward gay men and women yet. Particular targets of prejudice have been the "feminine" gay man and the "masculine" gay woman, and the man or woman who seems to change genders easily.

Berdaches are men and women whom Roscoe describes as belonging to third and fourth gender roles. Roscoe, who won the Margaret Mead Award for his previous book, *The Zuni Man-Woman*, shows that he is just as probing as was Mead herself in his search for the meaning of gender in our personal and cultural lives. In a section of *Changing Ones* titled "Gender without Sex," he explains that the concept of gender, which a contemporary expert has "traced to the 'gender identity' research of the psychoanalyst Robert Stoller in the 1950s," is etymologically derived from the Latin *genus* (kind, sort, class) and "is widely used today to distinguish socially constructed roles and cultural representations from biological sex."[82] But he notes that in practice the concept continues to be linked to a traditional, binary conception of sex, as in the comment he quotes from a 1981 essay by Harriet Whitehead:

> A social gender dichotomy is present in all known societies in the sense that everywhere anatomic sexual differences observable at birth are used to start tracking the newborn in one of the other of two social role complexes. This minimal pegging of social roles and relationships to observable anatomic sex differences is what creates what we call a "gender dichotomy" in the first place.[83]

And Roscoe points out that even sex, in many American Indian cultures, was a "social construction on the behaviors of mothers and midwives." He says that the challenge in interpreting these cultures (and, through their examples, our own) is "to define sex without presupposing the naturalness of its forms and to define gender without reducing it to a reiteration of sex."[84]

Further, those physical differences that are part of a culture's gender categories may not be constructed as dichotomous or fixed, or viewed as determinants of social behavior. By extension, the presence of multiple

---

82 Roscoe, *Changing Ones*, 123.
83 Harriet Whitehead, as quoted in Roscoe, 124.
84 Will Roscoe, *Changing Ones*, 127.

genders does not require belief in the existence of three or more physical sexes, but, minimally, a view of physical differences as unfixed, or insufficient on their own to establish gender, or simply less important than individual or social factors, such as occupational preference, behavior and temperament, religious experiences, and so forth.

In this view, gender categories are both "models of" difference (to borrow Clifford Geertz's terminology) and "models for difference." They are used not only to explain the world, but they also serve as templates and instructions for gender-specific behavior and temperament, sexuality, kinship, and interpersonal roles, occupation, and religious roles. For individuals, gender identities function as the prerequisite for acquisition of other identities and roles. They are "total social phenomena" in Marcel Mauss' terms. A wide range of institutions and beliefs find simultaneous expression through them, a characteristic that distinguishes gender roles from other social statuses.[85]

All this might seem elemental, but its emphasis on the spirit, rather than the matter, in gender remains an assumption-challenging view even today. As Roscoe puts it:

> The evidence of multiple genders in North America offers support for the theory of social constructionism, which maintains that gender roles, sexualities, and identities are not natural, essential, or universal, but constructed by social processes and discourse. At the same time, it challenges certain assumptions of recent work in postmodern cultural studies, feminism and queer theory. These include assumptions that "sex" and "gender" are relevant categories in all societies and that sexuality and gender are (always) analytically distinguishable; that sexes and genders are binary and dichotomous and that, by extension only heterosexuality or the attraction between opposites is natural; that ideology and cultural beliefs regarding gender are always essentialist, which gender identities and sexualities are always constructed; and that the fluidity of human desire and the ambiguities of human categories makes stable identities and cultural continuity impossible. All of

---

85 Will Roscoe, *Changing Ones*, 127.

these assumptions are called into question by the example of native multiple genders.[86]

Roscoe's research into the lives of male and female berdaches makes clear that "native beliefs about gender and sexuality were avowedly constructionist, acknowledging the malleability of human desire and identity," yet at the same time the essential mystery and force of identity as an organizing factor for spirit are revealed: "North American multiple genders emerge as roles with great historical depth and continuity, with parallels in societies worldwide." Male berdache roles, he writes, "have been documented in every region of North America"; female roles "appear to be concentrated among groups west of the Rocky Mountains."[87]

The first half of this fine book is a carefully written history of the tribes and the berdaches. We are shown the life of the tribes, and in his careful research, Roscoe reproduces notes the explorers left dealing with their impressions of the berdaches. This is a scholarly book, but I had a hard time putting it down, because the scholarship is written from the heart.

Roscoe tells us that the term *two spirits* is beginning to replace the term *berdache*, and it is one that, as a Jungian analyst, I like better. It feels very Jungian to carry the opposites within oneself. I have often discovered that the gay man or lesbian woman truly are of two spirits. When I was much younger, getting introduced to Jungian thought as an analysand wife of a prominent analyst, the Jungian formulation of homosexuality seemed to be that the gay person was *identified* with the masculine or feminine and thus not in relation to anima or animus and therefore unable to individuate, since the anima or animus needed to be accessed to provide the bridge to the Self. For many Jungian analysts, therefore, homosexuality was a problem that needed fixing, if individuation was to proceed. I think the first person in my life who ever made an argument against that opinion was Dr. John Beebe, and the second person was my late son, Carl Frantz.

In his own challenge to the ignorance many psychologists still bring to the study of homosexual identity, Roscoe studies the history and the

---

86 Roscoe, *Changing Ones*, 5.
87 Roscoe, *Changing Ones*, 74.

mores of many, many tribal customs regarding the berdaches. Roscoe's title *Changing Ones* comes directly from the Native American idea of the mysterious transformation of male to female (and vice versa). The vibrant cover of his book depicts two Hopi dolls, called *warrior maidens*. Berdache males worked alongside the women, stringing beads and making rugs and clothing, and yet also went into battle with their brothers. These berdaches sometimes lived with men and were often considered their wives. Usually, their teepees were the most beautiful of any of the tribe, and other men often slept with berdaches to give themselves strength and courage.

The strength and courage of the berdaches was prized, as was their exceptional ability in the area of pottery and weaving. One example of the most famous weavers was Hastffn Klah, whose work is depicted in the book. Through his ethnological and anthropological research, Roscoe clearly illustrates that berdaches were gifted in shamanic practices and in healing rituals.

Berdache, a word imported by French explorers, is from a Persian word that "referred to a young captive or slave (male or female)." Roscoe carefully traces the etymology to the "Indo-European root which means to strike or wound, from which the Old Iranian *varta-*, 'seized, prisoner,' is derived." There are other meanings attributed to berdache, and it can be applied to women, but the one that has prevailed describes a male homosexual.

Roscoe's passion has taken him beyond the rediscovery of a single anthropological role for homosexual men into the realm of gender diversity. The idea of gender diversity is not original with him, and he cites references to the term in other investigations, but it has enabled him to document historically what this diversity can look like. The book contains numerous photographs of such famous Native American berdaches as the aforementioned Hastffn Klah, a male, as well as an unidentified female berdache. (She appears barebreasted in the photo, clad in a "man's breechcloth and men's bow guards on her wrist"; she poses proudly with her hand on her hip in a "masculine" pose.) Female berdaches reportedly rode into battle with the men and fought side by side. Some lived with women, and others married men and had children.

Roscoe gives us the groundwork of the Native American culture and his (sometimes chilling) account of the different explorers who, in their contact with the tribes, wrote of meeting men who dressed in women's clothing, were peaceful, and did women's work. That such men were prized by the tribe as having special shamanic talents and that their families were honored by the tribe to have such a son brought a lump to my throat. As a young mother, I had not felt honored by my community for having a gay child: quite the opposite, I felt shame. The reason for the shame was that in the 1950s women were the object of blame for having such a child. There was a great deal of psychobabble about the family constellation of strong mother–weak father that would produce such a child. I felt totally bewildered; my husband was a strong and present father and husband. I was told by my analyst that I was unconsciously bound to my son in a way that caused him to be effeminate. Yet he grew to be a masculine man, strong and artistic and intelligent. Clearly a model for such development was lacking in the culture in which I raised my son.

This book can be healing to a gay man's image of himself, because it shows that the berdache could be with the women and then mount a horse and do battle with the braves against the enemy, if necessary. And it offers this image to the gay man's family as well. If our family had been Native American, hundreds of years ago, and was honored by our tribe for bringing this unusual child into the community, how different all of our lives would have been. My husband and I and our daughter did our best not to pathologize his differentness and to enhance his life artistically, but we made so many terrible mistakes that we all suffered. Most of all, we felt we'd missed grasping what was normal in our situation.

In my inquiries into the childhood of gay men, I found that all the men with whom I spoke knew by five years old (and some, even younger) that they were "different." Some had a mother or a father who supported their uniqueness, and others had parents who stifled one or more of their spirits, by forcing conformity. Berdache children often grew up to be trained in the ways of medicine men and the shaman's art. Many contemporary gay children grow up hating gym (that place of gender conformity) and feeling left out of everyday schoolyard "fun" (again, so rigidly gendered). Not fitting in, they often hate themselves.

To someone with my background, *Changing Ones* seems an extraordinary book. The more I took it in, the more rage surfaced in me, not just at the injustice directed toward gay people, but regarding what we have historically done to our Native American brothers and sisters who were able to go way beyond the European's limited understanding of human ways. Alongside their loving attention to native animals and plants, Native Americans learned also to observe men and women, and they understood people on many levels, better than we do today. Quietly observing nature, they came to understand the berdache.

Would it surprise you to learn that as children some tribe members exhibited characteristics that made both parents and tribal leaders recognize they might grow up to be people of two spirits? Even in my own limited research, it has become clear that being gay begins in the womb. Roscoe illustrates this innateness with traditional stories of how the male berdache child was recognized. He was placed in a situation where he was allowed to choose male weapons or women's baskets. If he chose the basket, he would be raised to be a man of two spirits. (If, as he grew up, he decided this choice was not appropriate, he was free to change his mind.)

Those who are gay or have raised a gay son or daughter know that some gay children experience themselves as different very early, feeling the feminine or masculine qualities in themselves in an unusual and definite way. Other gay children find they fit in with other children, even though they feel attracted to the same sex when they go through puberty. Given my experience parenting a gay son, and my earlier adherence to the gender roles I was brought up with, the recognition of these alternatives to, and the ability to shift between, our culture's traditional gender roles feels healing and compelling.

Chapter 11

REDEMPTION

Originally published in *Psychological Perspectives*[88]

One morning at breakfast, sipping a lovely cup of decaffeinated coffee flavored with hazelnut soy cream, and having read the national, local, and state news, and the business section, I was happily reading my favorite sports page when a column headline leaped off of the page. "Goodbye Mike, Hello Christine." The byline was Mike Penner. What I read was more shocking than the idea that drugs may have been used in the Tour de France, more shocking than Barry Bonds' problems with supplements. Mike was telling his readers that he is finally acknowledging to himself and others that he is a transgender person. He spoke of the angst this decision has caused him and the people he loves. It was an honest confession about an immense change in his life. The gist of it was that he was taking a short leave, and when he returned to his column, he would have become Christine Daniels.

My first reaction was to marvel at the courage of Mike/Christine. I pictured his male readers gagging, spitting, and scratching their collective crotches, saying, "What the hell is going on? Mike is a *dame*?" And I hoped they would understand, but knew many of them wouldn't.

Often I have a meal at a small Mexican restaurant near my home and like to watch the waiters and especially the bartender as they animatedly talk among themselves about their bets on football and other sports. These are typical macho, testosterone-laden guys—men's men. How *could* they understand that a male journalist, who has worked for the

---

88   Gilda Frantz, "Redemption," *Psychological Perspectives* 51(1), (2008): 3-6.

Times for 23 years and is an athlete himself, would want to be a woman? I was wrong. I recently began an email exchange with Christine Daniels and she said that, out of some 600 messages responding to her column, only two or three were negative.

From earliest memory, she always wanted to be a girl and had fought it all of her life. And now, at age 49, she finally found the courage to go ahead with it after what must have been a supreme struggle. The column brought tears to my eyes as I wondered how she would be able to fit in with her fellow journalists and other colleagues. What about covering a sporting event, would she still hang out with the guys? She is now a beautiful, elegant-looking woman—how would they take to her sitting around with them as they'd done *before*? But once again my assumption was incorrect. She has received enormous support from fellow sports writers, from the staff of the *Los Angeles Times*, as well as from total strangers.

One of my favorite lines from Jung is that we don't change because we want to, we change because of *necessity*.[89] We change because we cannot live with our situation as it has been. It was clear that Christine HAD to do this.

I am the mother of a gay man who was gay since childhood and yet, when he came out, I fretted over his *choice*, wishing he could have made a better *choice*. Of course, eventually I realized it wasn't a choice, any more than Christine's transformation is about choice, but it took a long time for me to finally get it.

I didn't write to Christine after that column, because my heart was too full to even find the right words to say what I wanted to say. So I was silent. But I kept looking for her byline, hoping that she would get her job back and I could read her column again. Months later, I saw a large photo spread and a column that bore her name, and I knew that Christine Daniels was back. But Mike Penner was gone forever.

This issue of *Psychological Perspectives* has taken the theme of redemption, and the articles will make you think about what is being redeemed and what needs redeeming. There are a number of ways to interpret the word *redemption*. My trusty dictionary suggests one definition: to

---

89 C.G. Jung, "Development of Personality," CW 17.

redeem is *to fulfill an oath, a pledge, or a promise.* It is commonplace to think of redemption in relation to sinners or sinning, For me, its more positive meaning to fulfill an oath or a promise fits very well with Christine's story, or the story of anyone who has withheld something that they believe to be the core of their being or their true self. By literally becoming the woman she longed to be for a lifetime, Christine has redeemed the promise she whispered to herself long, long ago. I think that Christine Daniels has redeemed the lost and hidden feminine in herself in a way that few of us ever dream. It takes enormous courage to announce to the world that you are, at heart, a woman and not a man at all; it takes great courage to tell a brother or sister about this, let alone a parent. Recently Oprah Winfrey had a program all about gender changes in young people. A young woman of 21 and a young boy of 17 had both begun life as opposite genders. The little girl who became a boy never wanted to be a girl, and the lovely young woman had never wanted to be a boy. This is much more intense than wanting to wear pants and not dresses as a kid.

These weren't individuals at midlife, these were children who announced that they were no longer willing to be the gender to which they were born, and they found a way to get their parents' approval and help.

How many of us have dreamt of changing in a major way? Is that what a midlife crisis is about? Coming to a place in life where we realize that we have a limited time ahead and deciding to do what we had always wanted to do or be? But to change one's gender seems so impossible. Or did she change her gender? Does someone who has wanted to be a girl from earliest childhood change her gender or allow her gender to be what it is?

What does Christine's story mean psychologically? Does it speak to a deeper understanding that we have at this time to be able to empathize with a person who feels that his or her body is alien? Perhaps it hints at a wider, if not-so-conscious, grasp of the true nature of the masculine and feminine principles as fluid energies we all share in varying amounts.

Part 4

PSYCHOLOGICAL AND SPIRITUAL DEVELOPMENT

All the greatest and most important problems of life are fundamentally insoluble. They must be so, for they express the necessary polarity inherent in every self-regulating system. They can never be solved, but only outgrown.

—C.G. Jung[90]

---

90 C.G. Jung, "Commentary on 'The Secret of the Golden Flower,'" CW 13, ¶ 18.

Chapter 12

THE FLOWERING WOOD:
AN EXPLORATION OF INDIVIDUATION AND THE
INTEGRATION OF THE FEMININE PRINCIPLE

Originally published in Japanese
in the *Sanno Clinical Series*[91]

One of the most outstanding contributions Jung has made is his living demonstration of his concept of individuation. Those of you who have read his autobiography, *Memories, Dreams, Reflections* will understand what I mean by that remark. I have chosen the theme of individuation for my talk today because it is a subject I have pondered for a great deal of time.

I am honored to be speaking here today to colleagues who have traveled so far to learn about Jung's ideas, as interpreted by those of us who live and practice in the United States. Some years ago I heard Professor Hayao Kawai speak in Zürich about transference. He spoke in such a unique way about concepts that I knew and had studied, that I was able to feel the three types of transference he was describing and to understand the various combinations of transference that were possible. I was so impressed by his scholarship *and* his humor that I invited Dr. Kawai to speak at the C.G. Jung Institute here in Los Angeles, and he has since been invited back twice. I felt that one day there might be a dialogue between Jungians, East and West, and now that you are here, thanks to the efforts and energies of Dr. Ogawa and others, the dialogue I hoped for is a reality. I also want to thank Mrs. Sachiko Reece for kindly trans-

---

91   Originally published in Japanese in the *Sanno Clinical Series*, 1987.

lating my talk for those of you who need a translation. Mrs. Reece is a Jungian colleague whose work and ideas are respected. I hope she will add her comments as to how this material resonates within her. Being Japanese and living in the West, she is in the unique position to express something of both realities.

My talk covers the following points: first, a look at individuation and what that means; second, I will tell the story of *The Adventures of Pinocchio*, a children's fairy tale, as a way of illustrating the process; and finally I will introduce the feminine archetype in the form of Isis, Wisdom, and the Blue Fairy as manifestations of the unconscious that are vital to individuation.

By *individuation* I mean that which is ineffable, unquenchable, and relentless within us in its desire for wholeness. In order to become whole, there is an enormous amount of living, suffering, loss, and change we must go through. We must recognize our shadow and its projections, on every level, inner and outer. Jung says that the goal of life is not perfection, it is wholeness. In order to come to that experience of being whole, we must recognize the inferior part of ourselves, that part that most of us disown or deny or try to run away from because it is so imperfect. Often in our dreams is a shadow figure represented by some kind of tough guy who threatens or frightens us, or someone who is very much our opposite and whom we dislike or don't respect. A woman who has always lived a proper but inhibited life dreamed of a brazen woman who was easy with men and who dressed in a flashy, "cheap" way. This figure was a shadow figure, symbolic of something within herself that she has denied, disliked, and/or rejected.

In his brilliant essay "Development of Personality"[92] Jung writes that the only thing that motivates us to change is *necessity*. This change is often preceded by an inner or outer fatality—something or someone of value that has died inside or outside of us. At such times dreams may contain symbols of the death of someone known or unknown to us. Other symbolic manifestations of the beginning of individuation can be dreams of houses being built or restored, a room or new wing being added to the house, or an entire section discovered that the dreamer never

---

92 C.G. Jung, CW 17.

knew existed. Another foreshadowing of individuation can be seen in the vision of a woman who had suffered a deep and irreplaceable loss. In the vision, her heart became the earth out of which a tiny new tree was growing. Tears watered this tree and eventually the earth/heart opened due to the growth of the new tree within her. This tree can be seen as a new self, a growing thing that she had never seen before. The water of her tears, her suffering, was necessary for her individuation.

If our ego consciousness does not change and grow as we mature physically, we will have the same consciousness we had as children. This truncated ego development is inappropriate and inadequate for the process of becoming whole.

When an "inner fatality" is experienced, we become isolated, segregated from the undifferentiated herd, a process similar to the process of mourning after a death in the family. This is the experience of depression. Depression is one way the unconscious brings us down into our depths to come face to face with what it is that we need to change. This can mean changing an attitude or self-image or something as basic to our further development as the work we do. Often as young people we choose a profession or work that will satisfy the ambitions and desires of our family. With the arrival of midlife, we may sense a time for reassessment, for remembering. A long, forgotten yearning reappears, unbidden and unwanted, perhaps in fantasies or in dreams. When this happens, it is as though a voice is beckoning us to follow. Occasionally we will listen and do something drastic, like quit our job or move or make an internal commitment to write poetry or paint, etc.

What is it, Jung asks, that causes us to choose our own way? He uses the expression *vocation*. Vocation originally meant "to be addressed by a voice." We tend to believe that only prophets or psychotics hear voices, but in order to traverse the long and untraveled road, we must listen to the inner voice of wisdom. It is as if we are destined to follow this inner conviction, this vocation. My dictionary tells me that "fate means divine decree." With only a slight stretch of the imagination, we might say that if one is addressed by a voice that makes a divine decree, then is there a choice?

It may be a holy or divine voice that urges us on, yet we have no guarantee that if we faithfully follow this inner voice, we will attain success in the worldly or outer sense. To the outer collective our journey may look, in fact, like a disaster. But do we have a real choice? Either we follow this voice or we commit "partial suicide." Jung calls the neurotic's fear of launching out into life "partial suicide" because something is not fully lived in order to hold back this drive, this instinct we have for wholeness.

The idea of vocation is not the property of the great or the famous. Nor is it limited to ancient prophets or to schizophrenics. The less conscious we are, the fainter the voice. The less conscious we are, the "smaller" is our personality. *Small*, in this instance, is equated with unconsciousness.

If our personality is small, then we are more prone to listening to the values of the collective and more prone to surrendering our own wholeness and dissolving into the wholeness of the group. Instead of being able to hear our own inner voice, we hear the voice of the group with its limitations, conventions, and collective attitudes. Vocation, then, becomes replaced by collective necessities. Jung writes:

> The achievement of personality means nothing less than the optimum development of the whole individual human being. It is impossible to foresee the endless variety of conditions that have to be fulfilled. A whole lifetime, in all its biological, social and spiritual aspects, is needed. "Personality" is an act of high courage flung in the face of life. The absolute affirmation of all that constitutes the individual it is surely the hardest task the modern mind has set itself.[93]

Why do we undertake this difficult journey? Because we desire happiness. The word *happy* derives from the same root as "fortune," and it means good luck. Happiness is connected to a spiritual sense of wholeness. When we are centered and whole, we feel happy, but that is not a constant in many of our lives. The Declaration of Independence grants all Americans the right to "the pursuit of happiness," but cannot guarantee our finding it. Nothing can guarantee that.

---

93 C.G. Jung, "The Development of Personality," CW 17, ¶ 289.

In an intuitive way, not readily explained by logic, I find the story of Pinocchio to be a wonderful illustration of individuation. *The Adventures of Pinocchio* was first published in Italy on July 7, 1881, by Carlo Lorenzini who used the pen name of C. Collodi. The story appeared in installments in a leading children's weekly, *Gironale per/Bambani*. C.G. Jung was almost six years old when this story first appeared.

The story begins with these words: "There was once upon a time a piece of wood. This wood was not valuable; it was only a common log like those that are burnt in winter in the stoves and fireplaces to make a cheerful blaze and warm the rooms." There is an ordinary and everyday quality to this log. It is available to anyone. The man who owned this log was a woodcarver named Mr. Cherry. Mr. Cherry was going to carve a leg for a table and began at once to use a sharp instrument on the log. No sooner did he do this than the log said, "Do not strike me so hard!" Mr. Cherry was shocked. The log had a voice. Almost at that moment, the door opens and in walks Geppetto, who also is a woodcarver. He asks for a piece of wood to make a puppet. Mr. Cherry is only too glad to get rid of this log.

Geppetto has dreams of fame and of making his fortune with his puppet, and he is lonely and childless. Marie-Louise von Franz writes that creation often begins when the gods are lonely. One might say that "in the beginning there was loneliness before anything existed upon the face of the earth."

Geppetto wanted to become a father and to create something special. He wanted to become famous. Striving for fame is part of the *prima materia* out of which one builds an individual life. It is precious stuff to be ambitious. Fame is what motivates him. This is not unlike the story of Genesis. Whereas in Genesis the Creator took a piece of common clay to create man, in our fairytale Geppetto uses wood to make a puppet. The Creator also had desires for what Adam and Eve might become if they had remained in the Garden. Because Geppetto was so eager to use Pinocchio for his own ends, it was even more important that Pinocchio individuate, that he rebel. Otherwise he would have been subsumed by Geppetto.

"The symbolism of tree, trunk, pillar, and stake is also determined by the nature of wood, which, is not only a product of growth but is also the matter, the *materia*, from which all things arise."[94] From this we understand that this elementary character is the material of transformation, like the prime matter that the alchemists used to turn lead into gold. It is the cradle and the casket. Jung gives us a fuller picture of what the figure of Geppetto might represent in this story:

> The archetype of the wise old man first appears in the father, being a personification of meaning and spirit in its procreative sense. The hero's father is often a master carpenter or some kind of artisan. According to an Arabian legend, Terah, the father of Abraham, was a master craftsman who could cut a shaft from any bit of wood, which means in Arabic usage that he was a begetter of excellent sons. . . . In fairy tales the hero's father is, more modestly, the traditional woodcutter. In the rig-Veda the world is hewn from a tree by the cosmic architect, Tvashtri.[95]

Geppetto takes the log home, puts it on his worktable, and begins to carve it. He hears a voice, which calls him Polendina. This is the name for a pudding made out of Indian corn. The image of Geppetto as food indicates that he will be both mother and father to the puppet and as such the source or all nourishment. Though absent at the beginning, the feminine comes into this story in the form of a divine being a little later on. Geppetto continues to be annoyed with Pinocchio, but seems not at all amazed at the fact that the wood can speak. No sooner does Geppetto carve Pinocchio than the puppet jumps off of the table and begins to run as fast as he can, even before his feet are fully formed. It soon becomes clear to Geppetto that he cannot control this puppet in any way.

This is an excellent picture of the early stage of ego development when there is no real destination, just energy! And, without the support of a real standpoint.

---

94 Erich Neumann, *The Great Mother*, 49.
95 C.G. Jung, "The Dual Mother," CW 5, ¶ 515.

Pinocchio has many adventures, which involve both helpful and wicked animals as well as kind and cruel people. Early in the tale he meets a Talking Cricket who is wise and full of good advice for Pinocchio. Cricket has lived in the room, where Pinocchio and Geppetto now live, for the past 100 years. He tells Pinocchio that he should be a "good boy and not rebel," but Pinocchio laughs, telling Cricket that he, Pinocchio, is the owner of the room now and that if he listens to Cricket, he will have the same fate as all other boys—namely, that he will have to go to school.

All Pinocchio wants to do is eat, drink, play, and have a good time. This attitude is one of grandiosity and inflatedness. Pinocchio doesn't think he needs education or any kind of guidance. He doesn't want to listen to anything that remotely resembles good advice. In fact, quite the opposite, he wants to avoid the fate of all good boys, which is to be taught. For our purposes that means he wants to avoid consciousness with its demands and limitations to the so-called good life. He wants to be a vagabond from morning to night.

When Cricket hears this, he pities Pinocchio—which so enrages the puppet that he smacks Cricket, killing him unintentionally. Pinocchio's attitude is appropriate for his age and development. If he listened to the *cricket-voice* at this time, he would not separate himself from the collective. This collective education would not educate him about suffering; it would repress him. To be a good boy meant that Pinocchio would lose his vitality, his thrust, and masculinity. Pinocchio needs to make mistakes, needs to have adventures, and needs to suffer. There are many times when Pinocchio thinks about Cricket's advice and wishes he had listened. By that time he has had adventures and has learned something about life and its pain. He is able to reflect, but when Cricket first advises him, he has not yet experienced the "inner fatality" that brings about change in a transformational way—and that is what the story of Pinocchio is about: transformation. He begins life as a wooden log, becomes a puppet, and eventually through his suffering, he becomes a real boy.

This is a good time to talk about wood as a symbol of the feminine principle. Wood represents the life force, that aspect of the tree that is both of the earth and of the spirit. It is the nurturer of fire, provider of

shelter for home and temple alike. Trees were worshiped as deities, and
wood has that divine quality also. Neumann says that the tree of life
is female: that it bears, transforms, and nourishes. It is protective and
gives shelter to birds by supporting their nests, but the tree trunk is also
a container wherein the spirit dwells as the soul resides in the body. The
female nature "of the tree is demonstrated in the fact that treetops and
trunk can give birth."[96]

In the Old Testament, Proverbs (8:22–24), we hear Wisdom speaking. Wisdom is Sophia, the feminine, an aspect of the Good Mother
and like the Blue Fairy who appears in the story of Pinocchio; she is a
manifestation of the unconscious, all wise and knowing, a guide into the
mysteries. Wisdom/Sophia describes herself this way:

> I was exalted like a cedar . . . and as a cypress tree upon the
> mountains of Hermon . . . I was exalted like a palm tree . . .
> and as a rose plant in Jerico . . . as a fair olive tree in a pleas-
> ant field . . . and grew up as a plain tree by the water . . . my
> branches are the branches of honour and grace . . . and my
> flowers are the fruit of honour and riches, . . . I am the mother
> of fair love . . . and fear . . . and knowledge . . . and holy hope
> . . . I therefore, being eternal, am given to all my children . . .
> which are chosen of him.[97]

Here we see Wisdom as tree, natural and green, bringing eternal life to
all her children, the mother of us all. And in Jung's words:

> As . . . the spirit of God, she brooded over the waters of the
> beginning. Like God, she has her throne in heaven . . . she
> is the mother-beloved, a reflection of Ishtar, the pagan city-
> goddess. . . . All these trees have from ancient times been
> symbols of . . . the mother-goddess. A holy tree always stood
> beside her altar on high places. Oaks . . . are oracle trees. God
> or angels are said to appear in or beside trees.[98]

---

96 Neumann, *The Great Mother*, 49.
97 C.G. Jung, "Answer to Job," CW 11, ¶ 610.
98 Jung, "Answer to Job," CW 11, ¶¶ 611-612.

By describing herself as having her throne in heaven, Wisdom brings up the image of Isis, whose name means "the seat" or "the throne." We know that the king gets his power from sitting upon the throne, that is, on the lap of the Great Mother.

The myth of Isis and Osiris has special meaning for me for reasons that are not altogether unrelated to this paper. I heard an Egyptian guide read the hieroglyphics off an ancient temple wall at Abydos some years ago, telling us the myth of Isis's journey to bring her husband Osiris back to life. The first time she did this, he had been dismembered by his brother and his body scattered all over Egypt. Wherever a part of him rested, there was fertility and growth. Isis found all the parts of his body except the phallus. With the help of her sister, she put Osiris back together again, carving a new phallus out of wood. When she had attached the new phallus, she coupled with Osiris and a child, Horus, was born of this union.

Hearing about her great devotion to her husband touched me deeply, but it was only recently that I was again reminded of Isis. This time it was the inner Isis, the direct experience of the archetype, that touched me. A statue I found in Egypt fell on my foot in a synchronistic accident. The statue broke a small bone in my foot, but the real "break" came when I began thinking about what it meant to have something that had been dead and lost become the means through which new life could be born.

Something that had been created by the widow, by the feminine, brought the possibility of new life, of renewal. By hitting my foot, the Isis archetype was constellated. It was then that I began seriously thinking about Pinocchio, a puppet made from wood. Could Osiris's wooden phallus have meaning here? Symbols of Isis appear throughout the Pinocchio story, both positive and negative manifestations: the enormous snake, fire that burns off Pinocchio's wooden feet, the knife that carves the wood into a puppet. She is the boat that casts Geppetto into the sea.

Isis is known as a sheltering goddess, with outstretched wings protecting her creatures like a mother hen with her chicks. Pinocchio meets the Blue Fairy as the tiny chick he liberates from her eggshell. He is hungry and wants to eat, but when he cracks the egg a bird flies out and away. This bird appears again and again as a white blackbird, an owl, a crow, woodpeckers, a pigeon, a falcon, and a parrot—each time as a spiritual and life-saving force in Pinocchio's life. The unconscious flies into our lives in dreams of birds, birds that bring us messages or carry us away from danger.

Isis/Blue Fairy is also present in the magical growth of Pinocchio's nose each time he tells a lie. Like a living branch, his nose grows longer each time he is untrue. This living tree quality, which produces growth in his nose, is again the presence of the Great Mother. It is the visible quality of his long nose connected with his lies that makes everyone aware of his untruths, and this visibility is a punishment for him. He cannot hide his true nature from anyone, least of all the Blue Fairy. The phallic quality of his nose is evident and his shadow is apparent for all to see.

The first time Pinocchio meets the Blue Fairy, she is a beautiful "child . . . [with] blue hair and a face as white as a waxen image; her eyes were closed and her hands were crossed on her breast . . . her voice seemed to come from the other world. . . . In this house there is no one. They are all dead." She tells him she has lived for 1,000 years. Isis/Blue Fairy/ Wisdom is in the land of the dead, that place of the tomb. "As goddess of the tomb, she rules over the world of the dead, but at the same time she governs the celestial world, whose luminaries are her eyes." This is the place of rebirth where we meet those aspects that are universal and timeless. Whenever Pinocchio meets the Blue Fairy, she saves him through her interventions and those of the animals, the instincts, who are her allies.

The Blue Fairy repeats, over and over again, that he should listen, not be a bad boy, etc., but although he loves her, he doesn't listen. This is how the unconscious speaks to us all through our lives, repeating over and over what we know to be true, but a great deal of pain must be encountered before we take that voice to heart. We are given many chances in life to wake up, to grasp what we know inside to be true, but like Pinocchio, we lie to ourselves by denying the inner voice the serious consideration it deserves.

The Blue Fairy is very wise. She appears as herself at different times or as a goat with blue wool and as a woman who gives Pinocchio water during one of his terrible trials. Blue is a color long associated with sky and sea and divinity. That it is the fairy's hair that is blue suggests that she would be the feminine spiritual ideal that stays in Pinocchio's thoughts. All during his trials he thinks about the Blue Fairy and wonders what she thinks of him or whether she forgives him.

Just before the end of the story Pinocchio has his final and most dangerous adventure. He learns that his Papa Geppetto has gone out to sea in a small boat and has disappeared. Pinocchio bravely swims out to sea and is subsequently swallowed by a sea monster, the Dogfish. The story continues in this way:

> When he [Pinocchio] came to himself after the shock [of being swallowed], he could not in the least imagine in what world he was. All around him it was quite dark, and the darkness was so black and so profound that it seemed to him that he had fallen head downward into an inkstand full of ink.

Pinocchio sees a little light in the distance and discovers that Geppetto has also been swallowed. Pinocchio experiences an *enantiodromia*: He undergoes a complete change and begins to show feelings and concern for his papa; he even stops lying. He tells Geppetto all that has happened to him during the time he was "lost" and then finds a way for them both to escape out of the mouth of the fish. Jung sees this battle to emerge from the belly of the fish as an "attempt to free the ego-consciousness from the deadly grip of the unconscious."[99] This is the time in Pinocchio's development when a profound change has to occur or his consciousness will remain swallowed up.

After escaping from the fish, Pinocchio begins to take care of his papa, sacrificing his own needs for his father's well-being. He goes to work and earns 40 pence, which he sacrifices to help the Blue Fairy when he learns that she is ill. He sees a friend doing the work of a mule and watches him nearly die from exhaustion. The friend is that part of Pinocchio that has to die in order for the transformation to be complete

---

99   Jung, "Dual Mother," CW 5, ¶ 539.

and for his ego consciousness to change and enlarge. Gradually Pinocchio begins to emerge as a feeling, caring person who thinks about others as well as himself.

Others in this case would be the masculine and feminine, which are becoming reconciled within him. He has begun to embrace the feminine as well as the masculine and to integrate the two. He now calls the Blue Fairy "Mama"; she has become a conscious part of him rather than a fleeting thought. When the feminine out of which he was born (the tree) becomes integrated, he can function as a real person, a real boy, and he becomes compassionate. Only when we become aware of the need for compassion do we become real, that is, conscious. Being "real" means to be a conscious individual.

By becoming real, Pinocchio hasn't lost the true quality of wood; he has lost the *rigidity* of wood. He no longer deserts true nature—indeed, he embraces it. What he ran from was himself, his own authority. As he begins to be more feeling, Pinocchio exemplifies the notion of "fidelity to the law of one's own being" that Jung spoke of earlier. That is what helping his father and the Blue Fairy/Isis/Wisdom/Mama means. He is prepared to be responsible to his higher self. His attitude is now different from the selfish, ego-centered puppet. Pinocchio has become an individual, one whose suffering has brought him consciousness and compassion.

What Jung means by *fidelity* is not faith but *trust*. Fidelity to the law of one's own being is a trust in this law, a loyal perseverance and confident hope—in short, an attitude that a religious person would hold toward God. Personality can never develop unless the individual choses his or her own way, consciously and with moral deliberation. Pinocchio now has such an attitude and is willing to serve those important spiritual values.

Pinocchio has a dream in which the Blue Fairy comes to him and forgives him his trespasses. She tells him that although he is not perfect, he is worthy of being a real boy, and she kisses him and he awakens. He can hardly believe his eyes. He is a beautiful boy in new clothes. His room is a lovely room, not the straw-roofed shack he previously occupied. He puts his hand in his pocket and finds a little ivory purse.

Inside the purse are 40 gold coins. Geppetto is back to his former health and is working at his woodcarver's trade. Everything is new, better, and special. This ending is a wonderful depiction of the reward of becoming a conscious person. The gold, the room, the clothes, and especially the transformation to becoming a real boy are the result of the enlargement of Pinocchio's personality. From a naughty child who could not hear or would not hear the voice of Wisdom within, he has grown into a real person. Who could wish for more?

I would like to close by sharing with you a favorite quote from Jung:

> Anyone who wants to know the human psyche would be better advised to bid farewell to his study and wander with human heart through the world. There, in the horrors of prisons, lunatic asylums and hospitals, in drab suburban pubs, in brothels and gambling halls, in the salons of the elegant, the stock exchanges, Socialist meetings, churches, revivalist gatherings and ecstatic sects, through love and hate, through the experience of passion in every form in his own body, he would reap richer stores of knowledge than text books a foot thick could give him, and he will know how to doctor the sick with real knowledge of the human soul.[100]

---

100 C.G. Jung, "New Paths in Psychology," CW 7, ¶ 409.

Chapter 13

RELATIVITY AND RELATIONSHIP

Originally published in *Psychological Perspectives*[101]

Thirty-three years ago I attended a conference in Rome, sponsored by the International Association for Analytical Psychology, a conference that still takes place every four years in different parts of the world, and has done so since the mid-twentieth century. Analysts such as Marie-Louise von Franz, Gerhard Adler, and C.A. Meier, along with other Jungian luminaries, presented original papers. Jung made an appearance at the very first conference in the early 1950s. In 1950 there were possibly 200 analysts in the entire world. Today they number in the thousands.

Although I wasn't at the first IAAP meeting, I had gone often to such meetings with my analyst husband, but now I was a newly certified analyst and was going to the conference in Europe for the first time on my own. Madame Tissot, friend of my late husband and a Swiss analyst who lived in Rome, arranged for me to receive the hospitality of an Italian psychiatrist. He had generously agreed for me to be his guest, so after I arrived in Rome I made my way across the city to his apartment. It turned out to be an adventure. The young doctor had a girlfriend who was staying with him for a few days, and after I found out that he also had a wife and children in a nearby suburb, I began to feel as though I was in a slightly off-key Italian comedy—*off-key* because I spoke no Ital-

---

101   Gilda Frantz, "Relativity and Relationship," *Psychological Perspectives* 54(1), (2011):1–4.

ian and the doctor and his girlfriend spoke very, very little English. And there were no subtitles.

We found our way around the language barrier by sign language, facial expressions, and an Italian–American dictionary. I gather some of my efforts to communicate were hilarious since the young couple tended to laugh a lot when I "spoke" to them. But I was grateful for the shelter they provided and didn't take it personally.

I attended the conference and felt very delighted to be in Rome, especially living with these young lovers. We'd drink stale, cold espresso every morning, she and I in our negligees and he in his boxer shorts. More and more I felt surely I was in a steamy Italian film and my role was of the slightly clueless accepting mother. I was probably 50 at the time and the young doctor was around 30. And let's not even talk about his wife and children at home.

The doctor's inamorata was in her early 20s, and not at all domestic; thus the stale coffee. At breakfast we sat on small wooden chairs in the tiny kitchen; they would speak rapid Italian and I would observe the scene. I had a great time. Later I would go downstairs and have breakfast at a tiny coffee bar near the apartment house. If I went out at night, my host waited up for me in a fatherly way, and although I was much older, he played the father very convincingly. One night I went to a party at the home of an Italian analyst and danced almost until dawn. I was tip-toeing in when my host greeted me, a scowl on his face. I felt 15 again.

When the conference ended and it was time for me to leave Rome, the lovers invited their closest friends to a dinner party in my honor. I invited one or two of my colleagues who had expressed curiosity about where I stayed while in Rome. On the wall of the entry hall, the lovers had framed a note I wrote them (courtesy of my Italian–American dictionary) and showed it to everyone who attended. The laughter was hilarious and I smiled wanly, wondering what the hell I'd written in dictionary Italian. I found out it was the lack of syntax, grammar, and spelling and the absence of verbs that gave them such guffaws.

The young doctor graciously invited me to lunch the day before my departure, and surprised me by how well he actually spoke English. I began to realize that it was a game he was playing not to use my language, and indeed it had made our conversations imaginative, brief, and limited. In the café having a glass of wine and a heavenly bowl of pasta, we actually had a conversation. It was mostly chit-chat and pleasantries, before it occurred to me to ask a question. "What do you feel is the most common problem you see in your patients?"

His reply was fast and full of heat. "It is the *mauther*. She is the *beegest* problem." Ah, yes, the Mother Problem. And we nodded in mutual agreement of what a problem that really was. What he was referring to wasn't the harsh mom or the critical mom. He meant that *anything* about the mother was a problem. The Italian mother was described as clinging, loving, demanding, nurturing, domineering, but not a bad mother, just the kind of mother who is too close to her grown sons and daughters. The Italian mother knew too well how her grown children should live their lives, and freely told them.

We in America might call her the archetypal mother, but in Italy she was considered more like a goddess and was treated like one. My host considered the mother a major problem in his own life as well as the lives of young men and women all throughout Italy.

He and I had a lively discussion, and it didn't miss my notice that I was a mother, too.

On the flight back home, I gave this meeting much thought. He was quite right, of course, since the mother is powerful and important in all of our lives. Present or absent, kind, mean, or indifferent, she dominates our growing up, our fears, and our understanding of the world around us. If we have a too-positive relationship with our mother, it can be just as difficult as a too-negative one. I recall reading about two sisters, both around age 60, who still lived at home with their mom and dad because the sisters loved their parents too much to leave them. Their mother apparently was an angel, all giving and sweet and loving, and their father was a prince—kind, generous, and handsome. They couldn't leave these parents—not good at all when the object of being a parent is to give one's children roots and wings. Or so I now think.

I thought about Glinda, the Good Witch, in the *Wizard of Oz*, who was so sweet and kind to Dorothy. She gave Dorothy the red shoes so that she could get back to Kansas. Or was it so that she could leave Oz and return to reality? Goddesses in my mythology books had tempers and tantrums, and turned people into trees or blinded them if they got too close.

So there is no winning in this story, not if a good mother and a negative mother did equal damage to their children. In the end it's all relative, isn't it?

Chapter 14

REFLECTIONS ON DISENFRANCHISEMENT

Originally published in *Psychological Perspectives*[102]

The last time I was invited to be a guest editor of *Psychological Perspectives* was in 1972. I felt it was time for a women's issue and Bill Walcott, the founding editor, said "Okay, do it." Now, twenty-four years later, I am again guest editor and honored to be asked. Without our planning a theme for this issue, some of the articles and stories deal with the experiences of those who are disenfranchised. I find this particular synchronicity startling. In 1972 our theme also focused on a group of individuals (women) who were disenfranchised.

Have we seen any progress in ameliorating the conditions that give rise to disenfranchisement? Not much. Creative individuals seem to accept disenfranchisement as part of their fate. They take for granted blows from people like Jesse Helms who oppose freedom of expression in art (Maplethorpe), and although they rail against his ideas, they are not foreign to those in the art world. People of color still struggle to find a rightful place in our society. The disenfranchisement of the homeless or handicapped individuals is another story. Their very lives depend upon whether they are seen in our society, whether they are given a chance to circulate among their fellow beings and have access to the basics of food and shelter. When I visited Japan in the 1980s, I never saw a physically handicapped person on the street or subway in the entire three weeks

---

102   Gilda Frantz, "Reflections on Disenfranchisement," *Psychological Perspectives* 34, (1996): 12-15.

of my visit. Why was this, I wondered? Did the Japanese culture reject those who were different? Do we?

Feeling different and rejected is a subject that finds its way into many analytical hours. Individuals in analysis often reveal bag-man or bag-woman fears that they will find themselves on the street, homeless and wandering around penniless and friendless. Such fears clearly show our deep-seated horror of being on the outer fringe of society, abandoned and alone. In an analytical setting we readily seek understanding of the basis of these fears in the need to accept and get to know the inferior, rejected contents within the psyche. But how many of us pause on the street to accord understanding to the bag-man or bag-woman?

Since the deaths of my son Carl Frantz and my granddaughter Ariel Katz, I have become compassionate, more willing to take a moment and give a street person a few words along with the dollar I put into his or her hand. Standing outside the Music Center several months ago, I said "How are things going" to a man who was clearly homeless. In response to my question, he asked me to touch him, adding that he had not felt the touch of a hand in over a year. He was so sincere, so intelligent and related, that I put my hand on his shoulder and took his hand in mine for a brief moment. We both felt better afterward. But I had to go through two profound experiences of grief and loss that further human-ized me so that I could respond to such a request.

Why it is so difficult for the collective to accept uniqueness and dif-ference? Emerson wrote that society not only does *not* reward us for being an individual, on the contrary, it punishes us.

I was born to parents from Eastern Europe and am a first-generation American. Also, I was raised in a single-parent household, which by itself, in the early 1930s, singled us out as being "different." There were other things that set me apart from my classmates. We were very poor and moved a lot, so that I attended many schools and was always the "new kid" in class. On the most mundane of levels, even the food we ate made us different. As treats for me, my mother would render chicken skin into what she called *gribbenes*, a fatty, crispy morsel eaten on a slice of rye bread smeared with the fat that had congealed after rendering and sprinkled with salt; or a slice of rye bread, thick with sweet butter, its crust rubbed with a cut clove of raw garlic that imparted a stinging and pungent flavor to the bread. None of my friends ever ate this kind of food.

During the Depression years many people were poor—and also different—and what made those years special to me was that we were all in the same boat. Being out of work or poor wasn't so much an indication that one was a failure but only unlucky. I heard a lot in those days about luck. Now I see Lady Luck as another incarnation of the goddesses of fate.

These memories of times past make me ask, what has happened to our society that being different has become so stigmatized? I recall as a child knowing people who, though mentally challenged, worked productively in small "mom-and-pop" grocery stores, laboriously and meticulously performing their assigned tasks. Those clerks had a job and a place in their community. There were neighborhoods in those days and a feeling of community, allowing "eccentrics" and different people to feel contained, much like in the villages of Europe. Now people who are visibly different stay at home and come out only to pick up mail or cash a check, so that they aren't subjected to stares and snickers. Some of those who looked different in my childhood were "foreign" and some had been disfigured by accidents—but they were all part of my everyday life. In those days we weren't aware of having to look like everyone else or dress like everyone else or think like everyone else.

The United States of America, a nation founded by unwanted, unconventional people, is quite intolerant of individuals who veer from the so-called norm. And we are not alone. Many cultures consider banishment the proper punishment for those who break the traditions of their village or town or religious circle, be they European or African or Asian. I think of individuals who are born gay and spend the rest of their lives living under a stigma simply by being who they are, who they were born to be. Doesn't that sound barbaric?

Now research is beginning to show that being gay isn't a matter of choice or lifestyle. What does this imply for the future? During the stage of pregnancy fathers and mothers can choose to acknowledge that it is possible to have a gay child and be able to prepare for this blessed event.

Because it is blessed. Gay men and lesbian women have the dual delight of being one gender and understanding the nature of the other. Instead of being considered poor imitations of males or females, gay and lesbian individuals will be respected for carrying both sets of qualities.

I often ask people who seek analysis if they consider themselves to be the different one in their family; most often the answer is in the affirmative. Being the different one in a family can be very difficult. I have worked with artists who came from families that didn't value anything but making money—*big* money. Art and culture were viewed as worthless. When such a child is born into such an environment, it can be the work of a lifetime to feel value in one's chosen path. One artist's mother, upon being told by her son, who was a classically trained fine arts painter, that his paintings had sold out on the opening day of his exhibit, uttered, "So, how much did you make?" She hadn't a clue as to how unusual it is to sell all of one's paintings on opening day and that *that* was the amazing thing, not how much money the paintings had netted. But this was her only way of relating to how important the event was to her son.

This attitude is prevalent in our culture. When we hear about new films, the gross box office for opening day is as important as the content of the film. Has this always been so? Am I so different that I am still interested in the deeper value of culture rather than in what a film or book has grossed? One can see how focusing on how much money a film makes, when juxtaposed with the search for food and shelter, might intensify one's sense of alienation—of being on the outside, not even able to *look* inside.

In the final stages of production for this issue, I found myself becoming even more aware of issues of disenfranchisement within my community. I experienced this heightened awareness in a number of ways, but none as unexpected as during the performance of the *Cirque du Soleil*. Prepared to feel the soaring exuberence I'd experienced at previous performances over the years, I was disconcerted to sense an undertow, a tug downward, as the program unfolded. Even as the performers and clowns created spectacular magic as always, a deeper, more somber message was clearly present. With this issue of the journal fresh in my mind, I began to wonder if the circus had a similar theme. Not really believing a commercial venture would make such a heart-based choice, I whispered to my companion, "I think the theme is disenfranchisement."

During intermission, I scanned the program for the information on the name of this season's show: "*Quidam.*" Amidst the captivating glimpses of what lay ahead for us under the Big Top, I was astonished to find these words:

> *Quidam,* a nameless passerby,
> a solitary figure lingering on a street corner,
> a person rushing past,
> a person who lives lost amidst the crowd
> in an all-too-anonymous society.
> A soul that cries out, dreams and sings within us all.
> To that soul, *Cirque du Soleil* pays homage.

As do we.

Part 5

AGING

Personality is a seed that can only develop by slow stages throughout life. There is no personality without definiteness, wholeness, and ripeness. These three qualities cannot and should not be expected of the child, as they would rob it of childhood.

—C.G. Jung[103]

103   C.G. Jung, "The Development of the Personality," CW 17, ¶ 288.

Chapter 15

BEING AGELESS: THE VERY SOUL OF BEAUTY

Originally published in *Psychological Perspectives*[104]

It is the relationship to the Self that brings us beauty in old age, not the pots of face cream and powder, plastic surgery, or skin peels—although I'm sure each does a fine superficial job. Beauty in old age is the evidence of a relationship to the Self and the ego's developing acceptance of its now rapidly diminishing role. As we age, the ego has to learn to take a back seat more and more and allow the illumination of the greater Self to lead the way. Because the ego always wants to take credit for everything, this is something of a struggle, but struggle or no, it is worth trying to live life that way on a daily basis. The commitment I'm referring to isn't like going on a diet, getting stringent about not eating sugar or fat, then lapsing into one's old ways as soon as our will power is tired of the sacrifice. I'm speaking about the relationship to the Self that is unwavering and unchanging. This relationship brings light to our eyes and a kind of serenity that creates the look of beauty in an old person.

The most essential part of us is ageless. That said, how do we prepare for old age? If we don't prepare for old age, we feel raped by it. Aging is like a journey to a foreign land, and like any other journey, sometimes we wonder what to take on this trip which is leading us to the end of life as we know it. I suggest that a good beginning would be to take as few outer things as possible. In fact, for the trip into old age, the last thing you want to do is to take too much with you. Only what is essential

---

104   Gilda Frantz, "Being Ageless: The Very Soul of Beauty," *Psychological Perspectives* 50(1), (2007): 31–51.

belongs in old age. This is one journey where it pays to leave some things behind. I am going to discuss a few things necessary for this journey, the great and ultimate destination for all whose fate it is to live long enough to be called old.

What is *agelessness*? We all know someone who seems eternally young in spirit, and we often wonder how does he or she do it. I have come to understand that to be ageless we must each live our lives as though life is eternal, and quixotically we must be prepared for our death. It is in the reconciliation of opposites that we find the very soul of beauty in agelessness. Agelessness involves being *spiritually alive*. When we feel alive, when we have curiosity about life with all its mysteries and stay deeply connected to our soul, we are, in fact, ageless. If we are connected to our soul and have that rich sense of being alive, it is then that we are aware of the reality of death. In other words, we live with these opposing forces and reconcile ourselves to the reality that as sweet as life is, our soul will one day leave the body and the body will die. But before that happens, we have work to do.

In *Body and Soul,* Albert Kreinheder[105] wrote about the need to prepare for what he calls capital DEATH: "One of the serious conditions that older people often have is death anxiety. This is a real killer, a self-fulfilling prophecy. Paradoxically those who want to live well have to learn to die well."

He makes reference to the late beloved San Francisco analyst, Dr. Jo Wheelwright, who told Kreinheder that ever since he was 35 years old, a day hadn't gone by that he hadn't thought of his own death. When the time came for Dr. Wheelwright to die, he did die well. As full of life as he was—and his energy and vitality are well known—he was able at the right time to *let go*. But he had to practice for a long time. He was in his 90s when he died.

Kreinheder continues: "Once a person becomes 65 or 70, if not before, there is a considerable interest in longevity. We never seem quite ready to die. Maybe later, but not yet, please. . . . Thoughts of death and the preparation for death are very important because they put our lives in *truer perspective*."[106]

---

105 Albert Kreinheder, *Body and Soul: The Other Side of Illness,* 120.
106 Kreinheder, *Body and Soul,* 120-121, emphasis added.

In an active imagination, Kreinheder's inner guide said: "The object of healing is not to stay alive. The object of healing is to become more whole. Death is the final healing."[107] Active imagination is a way of accessing inner figures that can provide us with the kind of wisdom that isn't available to us through the ego but has to come through an archetype. That said, if our wish is to become whole, we need to begin to rid ourselves of some of the baggage we have been carrying around for a lifetime. We will die with it or without it, but if we examine what needs to be left behind, it will make this transition all the easier.

Related to this subject, Marie-Louise von Franz wrote: "Jung stresses that it is of great importance for the aging person to acquaint himself with the possibility of death."[108] I looked up the word *acquaint* in my *American Heritage Dictionary*; it comes from the root *to know* and means to make familiar, to inform. In other words, we need to be informed about death and get to know it. Knowing about the reality of death becomes the most important part of growing old. For me it may involve putting my hand on my arm or shoulder and saying to my body, "One day you will no longer exist," and really allowing that to sink in.

Once I awoke in the middle of the night from a dream and sat bolt upright in bed with that very thought. It is a lot to take in, that this flesh, these bones, this brain will be no longer. Or while at a family party, seeing the younger relatives with their even younger children and babies, I may say to myself, "One day they will be the older generation and I will be replaced," and feel good about it. We move on to make room for those coming up. That, to me, feels like a good thing. "Hello, my name is Gilda and I'd like to get to know you." I stick my hand out to greet death, and it is acknowledged for a brief moment, and I feel the reality of death and know I have to stay informed about this new acquaintance. I've known very old people who have seen everyone they knew die and wonder why death has forsaken them. For them death is a friend who has forgotten them, and they look forward to seeing death appear. In these situations the body becomes a prison from which they want to escape. Usually these men and women are bedridden and in their 90s or older.

---

107 Kreinheder, *Body and Soul*, 121.
108 Marie-Louise von Franz, *On Dreams and Death*, x.

Acquainting oneself with the notion of death is a process, not unlike learning about sex when you are a kid. When you are young, you need to hear about sex often to really understand that mystery, and when we are old, we have the same need in relation to death. Jung brings another dimension to this discussion:

> We ought to have a myth about death, for reason shows us nothing but the dark pit into which we are descending. Myth, however, can conjure up other images for us, helpful and enriching pictures of life in the land of the dead. If we believe in them, or greet them with some measure of credence, we are being just as right or wrong as someone who does not believe in them. But while the man who dispairs marches toward nothingness, the one who has placed his faith in the archetype follows the tracks of life and *lives right into his death*. Both, to be sure, remain in uncertainty, but one lives against his instincts, the other with them.[109]

Agelessness is the ability to live with passion until the moment we die. We all know people who are living but not alive. When I was in India many years ago, the poorest people living in battered, used oil barrels on the streets of Calcutta had a light in their eyes; it wasn't a twinkle, it was a *light*. I don't know if that light exists today, knowing the severe poverty and sickness that prevail throughout that part of the world. To our Western way of thinking, India is a place where nothing works, which means that the most minor task takes forever to accomplish, and red tape is legendary. On that same trip to India, I met a poor man in Agra, carefully tending the roses at dawn in the hotel rose garden, who showed more compassion than I had ever before experienced from a stranger.

When I returned to this country, it became clear to me that although systems work in our country and are performed in record time, there was no light in people's eyes as they went through their tasks. India had introduced me to something vital: the experience of how the spirit within us is made manifest by constant contact with it. This lack of spirit was so obvious at the airport as I went through customs here at home, that

---

109 C.G. Jung, *MDR*, 306.

the realization of it caused me to stay inside my house for a week upon my return due to culture shock in reverse.

What made the difference, I wondered, thinking about the radiance in the poor Indian. I came to the conclusion that it had to do with the spirit. He experiences something many of us have no connection to: namely, being spiritually related to something larger than his own being. The best answer I could find was that the commonest Indian has a belief in a living god or goddess; that he or she believes in reincarnation and has the expectation that in his or her next life, things might be different. This living relationship to the gods nurtures the spirit even though the body suffers.

What the Indian man had was a living myth about life and death that suited him and the belief that something better awaited him in the beyond. To the Indian, the gods are alive and worshipped daily. His gods are with him all the time. He adorns temples and often dances and plays music to celebrate the goddess. There is a tempo and love that abound in relation to the spiritual side of life; they are one. In India the opposites are very close together. You can see a wedding procession gaily coming toward a temple and see a corpse being carried off for cremation, all within moments of one another.

Jung notes: "In cases where the dreamer has illusions about his approaching death or is unaware of its closeness, dreams may even indicate this fact quite brutally and mercilessly."[110] Dr. Kreinheder had such a dream some years before he became old or ill. In the dream he was required to dig his own grave, but somehow he kept putting it off. He awoke from that dream feeling that obviously he had better take care of some things. He contacted a lawyer and drew up a living trust and above all tried harder to be in touch with his soul.

Any of us who has survived a serious illness or a catastrophe has not forgotten how it felt to be on the very edge of life. Even though it is scary, there is also a great challenge in living through something, or surviving an event, that calls upon us to be as sharp and alive as we have ever been. Sometimes those moments of serious threat to our well-being make us aware of the excitement of living life in a fuller, richer way. We

---

110   as cited in von Franz, *On Dreams and Death*, 1984, ix.

become aware of what is really important to worry about and fret over, and finally we know what does and doesn't matter in our lives. When my sister was undergoing treatments for breast cancer in the late 1960s, she told me that this would be the most interesting experience of her life, if only it wasn't fatal. She was 52.

Agelessness involves living with the awareness of death as a natural sweetener of life. The knowledge of the end of our physical existence makes time with loved ones, or looking at a sunset or watching a sunrise, all the sweeter. This greater knowledge of the transitory nature of life isn't morbid, it's practical. Many of us would like time to stand still, so we could stay where we are. If we don't plan for the end of our lives, however, we won't be really living. We'll be worrying about everything. I believe in getting a burial plot (or making arrangements for cremation), drawing up a will, and preparing all the needed documents—and then forgetting about it. By "forgetting about it" I mean to take a deep breath and recognize that this part of our work is complete.

Because of certain experiences in my life, I do feel that there is some continuum of life after death. What that "life" is, is unknown to me and will remain so while I am among the living, but that is my belief. Jung remarked in an interview that the unconscious acts as though life doesn't come to an end. In fact, dreams of very old people who are dying can be bright, alive, and often do not depict themes that foretell the end of life. Jung developed the notion that the *unconscious* believes in some kind of continuation of life after death.

Adaptability—staying flexible—is very important to retain as we age. The ability to flex: Pack your bag to take with you into old age. The big danger in old age is that we can become rigid. I like my routines but am also convinced that I need to shake myself out of them every once in a while. We need to learn a new language to live in a foreign country in old age so we don't become stiff. When traveling in a foreign country, one needs to think about everything—language, currency, manners, and how to find a toilet. It is very rejuvenating to not always have the answer. But even if we don't travel to unfamiliar places, we can accomplish the same with how we think and to what we open our minds. Any new knowledge we learn has the same effect on the brain as going to unfamiliar places. New knowledge lubricates the brain, so to speak.

A friend who was dying last year wasn't able to let go and die peacefully until he found a way to say "Okay, I'm ready." And when he came to that place, he did let go. Before that he was angry and frustrated that he was dying because he had so much he still wanted to do. He was utterly young at heart. This is his story.

His wife called me to say that her husband was feeling very alone because his friends were not visiting him anymore. She reasoned that it was difficult for them to see him in this weakened state when they had known him as a man of action and strength. And he was loath to be seen this way as well. He was lonely for meaningful conversation, and his wife thought I might be able to give him that.

I have been associated with both loss and creativity for the 30 years I have been an analyst, so it wasn't surprising to be asked to visit an old friend who was ill and dying. I went as a visitor, not as an analyst, and looked forward to seeing this interesting and creative individual. We had known each other years before, when he was asked by my husband to build a beautiful wall out of old bricks for our patio. At that time I was a housewife and was able to observe him while he meditatively fitted one brick with another, wiping mortar with his fingers as he tapped the brick to be sure it would stay in place. I was a sculptor then and worked with clay, so he thought it natural to engage my talent by encouraging me to make gargoyles out of clay that would fit into the wall and function as water spouts for runoff from the upper part of the property. I sculpted these odd, grotesque faces, firing them in my kiln, and watched as he fit them into the used brick wall.

While he worked he was silent, but we talked when he took his coffee break, and I liked listening to his stories of the adventures he had experienced in building his own home. This project of his was taking years, which resulted in his entire family living out in the open until the roof went on.

Now it would be different, I thought, as I drove the winding, tree-canopied road to his house; he no longer was able to work, his house was complete, and he was spending his days alone reading and thinking. He is a very deep thinker, well read, able to express himself; it would be good to see him and talk. The fact that he was dying wasn't a concern, as

I had sat with friends and family before and found it moving to be part of the mystery that was to be my own experience one day.

His petite brunette wife, an attractive, delicate-appearing, seemingly nervous woman, opened the door and said she'd go tell him I was here. I waited in their hand-hewn living room, with its massive fireplace built by his own hands and interesting artifacts they had collected from who-knows-where. Everything in this house had his hand upon it. The cabinets, floors, walls, roof, stone fireplace—all built by his hand, assisted by friends and family for many years. The paneling on the walls had developed a warm patina over time. It was cozy.

He walked into the room, always thin but now a slender reed of a man, dressed in his worn jeans and still wearing the boots of a working man, though now the laces hung loosely. His ankles were swollen. He looked like the man I remembered: striking craggy profile, dazzlingly blue eyes, and sun-parched, lined skin now pale from too much time indoors. He was still a very handsome man, a Marlboro-man, sans the once ubiquitous cigarette. Instead he was attached to an oxygen tank by a long cord, the noisy contraption hidden somewhere in the house, silenced. I chose a comfortable chair, and he sat opposite me.

What was quickly apparent as he began to talk was that he was angry because of his fate. His doctor had told him that he didn't have long to live. From what I have experienced about fate, it simply befalls us. But he had been a heavy smoker, and I was pretty sure his illness had something to do with that habit, so was it fate or inevitability? He didn't want to die, at least not yet. He had work to do; there was life in him that still wanted to live and express itself. And he was angry with God. His voice had the timber and resonance and lilt of an Irish poet, though he was born in this country. When he spoke he ducked his head down and forward, like a hunting dog, sort of challenging his listener to debate.

I don't think I spoke much. Mostly I listened to this eloquent man. I felt that sitting with him, while he struggled with how to find a way to express his feelings and reconcile himself to the inevitability he was facing, was more important than my words.

Every week after that, I drove into the leaf-rich canyon feeling a sense of anticipation. Now his wife was absent, no longer coming to the door to greet me; she simply left it unlocked. I rang the bell, entered, and waited quietly until he came into the room, poured a cup of tea and sat down. I deeply enjoyed sitting with him as he wrestled with the dilemma he faced. His gnarled hands, folded in his lap, were cool and dry when we would shake hands in greeting. He noticed me looking at them and said with what sounded like regret, "They are clean for the first time in years—no concrete on them, nails not dirty." He missed being a part of the action, missed the long-time cronies he hung out with, missed being in life, and missed dirtying his hands. He expressed his anger quietly and his disappointment, too. He'd had the usual disappointments many of us face in life, of not feeling he'd attained the promise of his youth. As I listened to him, it occurred to me that although he couldn't work any longer, he could now turn to the occupation he had originally sought in life: being a poet/writer. "Why don't you write about what you are feeling," I suggested, adding, "it often helps me when I am in pain." To my surprise he took to the suggestion almost immediately.

When I returned the next week we dispensed with the cordiality and greetings as he waved me in with a sheaf of papers in his hand. Trembling, he began to read what he had written during the week. He wrote about his feelings, and I heard what sounded like a note of acceptance creep into his thoughts.

He never talked about being ill, even though he was attached to a tube that connected to an oxygen tank. He had devised a very long attachment to the tank so that he could freely roam about the house and not be confined to his bedroom. Even with this constant reminder of needing help to get air into his lungs, he didn't focus on being ill. We talked about the old days in college, when he learned he had a gift for placing stones just so. He described at length how he related to stone and how he could feel the spirit in each one. Life had been good to him to give him this gift; he was a poet and needed a way of supporting himself and his family, and working with stone turned out to become the poetry in his daily life—poetry he could express not with words but with his hands.

One week I noticed that something had changed. His face, always craggy and handsome, with Paul Newman-blue eyes and a redhead's complexion, now looked softer, as though some strain had gone out of him. Indeed it had. He said softly, "I want you to hear what I've written." I felt a sense of something profound about to happen and leaned forward in my chair as he read the short page of his handwritten scrawl. He had reconciled himself to death. It felt all right to him to decide to let go. It was his decision, and he had come to it himself, and now it was okay to allow this to happen. He felt ready.

I listened in a kind of awe because he didn't look ready to die. He was still dressed in street clothes for our visits; he fixed the water for his tea and often cooked or reheated his own meals. He didn't look the way other dying people looked, yet I knew when he said he was reconciled to the reality of death, that he would die soon.

When it was time for me to go, he kissed me lightly on the lips in a brotherly way and walked me to the door. He died a day or two later. He was 79.

This man's death and dying process is a superlative example of what it means to reconcile ourselves to our fate. He struggled with his idea of life, and death wasn't part of that idea. He treated death as an insult, not an inevitability, and the work he did was to understand and accept death as a natural part of life, much as the stones he placed so carefully and artfully. In fact, speaking with him about letting go, I remembered we had spoken about taking a stone from its natural place and moving it to serve another function in a wall or chimney. Life and death, it seemed to me, were a similar process: We are picked up and put in another setting. By making death a personal choice when we really have little choice does help us let go when we have to do so. That was his gift to himself.

Albert Kreinheder also died very peacefully. This peacefulness comes about, as I said earlier, by the work of reconciling the opposites within. During a difficult time in my own life, astrologer Thyrza Jones said to me that life has no opposite because the opposite of death is birth, not life. So if something has no opposite, then what? She was implying that life continues. Can you think of a word other than *birth* or *death* that is the opposite of life? I cannot find such a word.

When I was a child I knew Gracie, a woman with flaming red hair, a big bosom, and a rust-colored Pomeranian that was always sitting in her large, shapeless lap. I have no idea how old Gracie was. I never saw her stand up or walk, and I knew from my mother that she was ill in some way that kept her chair-bound most of the time. But she was full of exciting stories, and she fascinated me with her heavy makeup and huge necklaces of large, colored stones. She lived in a tent, whose only warmth was a tiny stove. The tent was part of a tent city created for the poor during the Great Depression. It was on a huge lot on a main thoroughfare; today a large market stands on that very place. As a young child I hadn't yet learned to distinguish rich from poor, and I loved visiting Gracie in her cozy tent and listening to her stories about her life in the opera. It all seemed so sacred and holy, sitting in her tent, often on a rainy Saturday when I would listen to the steady drip of rain as she told her stories. Images remain in my mind of a woman who was ageless and therefore fun to be around. This is a very important point: health, wealth, and position have nothing to do with agelessness. Agelessness is distinguished by the qualities of vitality and relatedness.

When I speak of agelessness, I mean a quality that belongs to certain men and women that is easily recognized. It is definitely not about physical attractiveness or how they dress or how much they do to make themselves "look" young. It isn't about looking young. It isn't about being "with it" in terms of style, although that may be part of the whole. Agelessness to me has to do with soul and spirit. It has to do not with the absence of suffering but how the person has integrated what suffering he or she has undergone. Suffering often opens us up and exposes places within ourselves that introduce us to our higher self.

We are speaking about one of the most important aspects of individuation here: the reconciliation of opposites. A person who is ageless has looked into him- or herself with honesty and found self-acceptance. If soul and spirit are visible and vital, then I would call the person ageless. To be ageless is to have a special quality of energy in which one's state of mind and relatedness are all tied together with some kind of passion or love. The ageless person is open and able to relate to people of any age, 2–100. There is a lot of love in a person who is ageless. Although agelessness is *not* about not getting stuck in the *puer* or *puella* archetype, it *is* about having more than a nodding acquaintance with one's inner child. As von Franz might say, ageless people are not childish, they are childlike. My father was a good example of agelessness. He took up painting when he was 80, something he had wanted to do all his life. At 90 he developed a tremor and had to stop painting the meticulous copper bowl and fruit still life that his night school art teacher had students paint, and he got a wider brush and began painting from his imagination. He took the challenge life handed him and reconciled himself to painting in a different way. It was the first time in his life he had painted images from the unconscious, and an anima figure emerged that made the work very compelling.

This is Stella's story. "Stella" was referred to me by her son, who knew that his mother needed help with feelings of depression. Into my office came a woman in her 70s, beautifully dressed, slender and lithe (she played tennis and golf), a woman who had beautiful features but wore an unhappy expression. She talked about her mother, who was in her 90s and had a tyrannical attitude toward her two daughters, one of whom lived near her and the other far away. This wasn't my first experience of an aging person talking about difficulties with a mother or father. Her story tumbled out of her, along with a mordant sense of humor and an obvious ability to laugh at herself. But much of what she said wasn't funny. We worked on her need for this very late separation from her mother—a separation that mainly took place within herself. After a while she was able to visit her mother without being reduced to nothingness by her mother's scathing remarks. This inner separation from the negative mother freed her to live and love the years that were left to *her*. And she did just that.

The following is a confession. "I have a new man in my life, I'm in love," I announced happily to my friends at tea. They collectively beamed and asked who he was. "Someone I've known for years and didn't properly appreciate. I've become reacquainted with him." Of course, they wanted to know his name. "His name is . . . (*here I drew out the words in a teasing way*) . . . Henry." They sighed and I continued, "Henry David Thoreau, and I am in love." A cloud of disappointment crossed their faces and then came their laughter. They all knew I meant it. I had come across a small book (its price of 75¢ still faintly visible in pencil). I found it on my bookshelves while looking for another book. My discovery initiated the renewal of a long-forgotten love.

I needed Henry now more than ever. It was from Henry that I learned about living alone, and it was from him that I learned how to live more simply. As we enter old age we need to remember to take a lover with us. He or she may be from the near or ancient past or of flesh and blood. Whichever it is, I for one, need love as I enter this new country, this uncharted land.

Why Thoreau, you might ask? He is accurately known as America's first ecologist. But Thoreau never reached old age—he was dead at age 44 in 1862. Thoreau knew about living large in a small way, and having chosen to live with less, he knew about giving things up, using what was essential, and not wasting resources (his own or nature's). That is what getting old is about. It is about what is essential, of giving up those many physical and material possessions and living with less and less on the outside and more and more on the inside, until we have made a transition.

In one of my active imaginations, a wise archetypal figure used the word *transition* instead of *death*. We make a transition, he said, from a world we know to another reality we know nothing about—yet, he went on, although there is something unknown about this place, it also seems familiar. This archetypal figure was very comforting. I now carry a mind-picture of the "other side." I have created a myth, as Jung suggested we do, of the beyond and it is no longer frightening. Death to me is a place beyond the stars, where spirits go when the body dies. In a sense, this next story is like a visit to the beyond.

On a lecture tour of Tokyo and Kyoto in the 1980s, I asked my hosts to give me three days to be alone before I met the academicians and psychologists from Kyoto's Jungian community. I had just come off a very long flight and felt a bit overwhelmed to be in Japan. I needed time to absorb the surroundings, the sounds of foreign words, and to just breathe in the new aroma of the city. My thoughtful hosts took me quite literally, and I was left utterly on my own in unfamiliar surroundings for three days and nights. Kyoto is a very beautiful city, ancient, noble, and timeless. After arranging with the concierge to give me a note that gave the address of my hotel and which said in Japanese, "This lady needs help. Please call her a taxi," I was able to go out on my own.

Awakening the first morning, I had breakfast and went for a walk through a bamboo forest—which, I learned, the local people run to as a place of safety in an earthquake (the close-growing bamboo provide stability). I walked down a path and found a road that went away from the hotel, in the process passing a special bush where tiny pieces of paper, containing handwritten prayers, were tied. It became a ritual for me to write my prayer on a small piece of paper and tie the paper to the plant on my way into town. I walked slowly, noticing, looking, sniffing the air. I saw a rice farmer in the classic peaked straw hat with cloth tied around his waist, a bandana at his neck to catch the sweat, wearing strange pants that to me seemed like a skirt with a band of material that went between his legs and tucked into his waistband. I saw pebbles on the ground and quivering leaves on the trees. I walked into a silent place that looked like a shrine, a temple, or many temples and sat myself on a shaded ancient wall listening to the silence. I breathed the damp morning air as I observed how green the mosses were and how moist everything felt, like being in a rainforest.

Other than the rice farmer, I didn't see another soul on my daily solitary walk. I felt safe on this road, yet I hadn't a clue where it would lead me. During my three-day self-imposed exile, I took this same path each morning, always wondering what I might see that day that I had missed the day before. By the time three days were up, I felt myself part of the landscape—still very much a stranger but with an appreciation of the beauty and unfamiliarity of my surroundings. I found a way to order food in a restaurant and ignored the giggles at my obviously strange pronunciation, enjoying that I had the courage to even utter a word in this very complex language. It was still strange and unfamiliar country, but now I felt ready to talk with colleagues. I felt I had walked the roads with a Thoreau-like attitude, noting everything and relating it to the larger meaning.

While writing one of the last entries in his journal, Thoreau was ill, indeed, not far from death. It was raining, and he had been housebound for quite a while, not able to walk around his beloved Walden. A surveyor by profession, he had walked all through Concord, Massachusetts, countless times in his life. Now he wasn't able to do that, so he sat at the window and looked out at the rain. A commentator said that at the end of his life that Thoreau became more factual and less poetic. You judge:

> After a violent easterly storm in the night, which clears up at noon (November 3, 1861), I notice that the surface of the railroad causeway, composed of gravel, is singularly marked, as if stratified by some slate rocks, on their edges, so that I can tell by a small fraction of a degree from what quarter the rain came. These lines as it were, of stratification, are perfectly parallel and straight as a ruler, diagonally across the flat surface of the causeway for its whole length. Behind each little pebble, as a protecting boulder, an eighth or a tenth of an inch in diameter, extends northwest a ridge of sand an inch or more, which it has protected from being washed away, while the heavy drops being driven almost horizontally have washed out a furrow on each side, and on all sides are these ridges, half an inch apart and perfectly parallel.
>
> All this is perfectly distinct to an observant eye, and yet could easily pass unnoticed by most. Thus each wind is self-registering.[111]

Thoreau understood that life's larger issues are seen in the observation of the small. And I believe *that* teaching in the deepest part of myself. We have the capacity to notice, in our old age, the smallest, most mundane observation and pluck meaning from it that will carry us through to the end of life.

When you pack for the journey into this last part of life, take your imagination and your dreams. Take your passions and your dearest vision and notice everything that will help you understand where and why you are here. Take as little as possible of those all-too-human feelings of having failed, leave behind your concern of a lack of accomplishment. Leave behind resentment. Maybe you didn't write that great novel or invent that never-before-seen tool.

---

111 Henry David Thoreau, *The Writings of Henry David Thoreau: Journal*, p. 346.

Now, in old age, or approaching old age, it is time for acceptance of our limitations. All that mulling about failure and lack of accomplishment acts to weigh us down on the journey. It isn't that one cannot write or invent in old age; in fact, one can. There used to be a saying that if you haven't published by the age of 40, you never will— but that isn't true anymore, so don't stop writing. I have a friend who, at 89, has just published her first book.

What you want to let go of is the demand *inside* yourself. You don't leave dreams behind, you leave the unreality of dreams that don't help you attain or achieve self-realization. Give yourself a little credit for what you have been able to do in life and keep on learning, moving, and evolving. What you need to shed are some of the responsibilities you have carried, the burden of "should" and "have to," so you can be more responsible for your actions toward yourself and others.

The most important things to leave behind are the most difficult to untangle: your projections. They are not yours exactly; they are activated not by you, the ego, but by the unconscious. This understanding will afford you the opportunity to have more clarity about who you are and who you are not. As you withdraw projections, one by one, you will feel more spacious on this trip, as though you have checked a too-heavy suitcase at the train station. What a relief this is . . . one by one, remember, not a wholesale letting go. After all, you are aging, not dropping off the edge of a cliff and having your life flash before your eyes. So there is no wholesale letting go, just a one-by-one discarding of how you have seen people and how you've seen yourself. *Whew*, what a relief, what a lightening of a burden.

Take heart at what you have accomplished and what you are still accomplishing. When we take stock of our lives, as we do as we become old, it is very important to recognize how it has gone: how we have prevailed over difficult times and, with God's help, found a way to surmount our troubles. It is no small accomplishment to have lived a life, and we need to honor that. I had a dream in my 50s about being on a train en route to "somewhere," and it was time to get off at my stop. I had too much baggage, which I struggled to handle by myself as I tried to haul the bags and myself off the train (the porters were preoccupied with other tasks). I had to leave all but one bag behind so I wouldn't miss my stop. As I stood on the landing watching the train move off, I experienced regret as well as relief. It has taken me to my current age to dispose of some of that stuff I've been dragging around for a lifetime.

This next story is about what we hang on to. Meditation master Ram Dass realized one day that every time he relocated, he took boxes with him that he hadn't looked into for years. Finally he decided to have a ritual and burn those boxes, but before doing so, he would take a look inside and see to what he had been attached. In one box he saw his bar mitzvah certificate, in another were books he had long forgotten, in another pictures of a time past, and so forth. Satisfied, he then created a great pile of all the boxes and set a match to them and watched them burn. It was a joyous celebration. In retrospect, he let go of the boxes, not the memories, because here he was years later writing about the stuff in those boxes. He hadn't lost touch with the content, only with the physical stuff. So it should be for those of us lucky enough to even be able to contemplate getting old. We will relieve ourselves of our complexes and illusions and projections, but we will not forget them, because to forget is to become unconscious once again.

Old age is a time to give things away, not to accumulate more. I remember always that matter and material are related to *mater*, the mother, and the more we are attached to matter, the more we are attached to the Great Mother in an unconscious way, and the more we serve her in mundane ways. A better way to serve the Great Mother in old age is to communicate with her, to learn from her, to honor her as we move toward joining her in the not-so-distant future. We are on the brink of the eternal, the brink of joining the community of archetypes, as we leave the land of the known. The journey from the known to the unknown is a short distance, but it takes a lifetime to accomplish.

Another important piece of baggage to leave behind us as we go on this journey is regret. We all have regrets about what we have done or what we haven't done. A major regret of mine is the kind of mother I was to my children. That regret is harder to leave behind than things I personally haven't accomplished. I have come to terms with those already. Either I have done it or it will not get done. That I can handle, but not having been the mother my children needed is nothing I can remedy in this lifetime, and it sticks in my heart. Perhaps after this confession I may be able to let it go . . . maybe. But whenever you can, let go of regret; it does you no good. And it is a shame to take regret to the end of one's life. I'm still working on it.

The desire to find meaning in our life comes to us directly from the Self. Finding meaning is how the Self realizes itself. There is an instinct in us for creation and procreation; for play; for self-preservation and survival; and an instinct for spiritual development. Add to that list the instinct for finding meaning and for higher consciousness. The desire for meaning burns like a flame in each of us, and my wish is that someday that flame will become a light in us all.

The Self is a directing influence in our lives. It has been called "the great arranger" because it seems that the Self arranges life in order to bring about self-realization. We feel the directing influence of the Self and synchronicity presenting themselves at various times in our lives.

The combination of suffering and seeking creates the circumstance of finding meaning in life. As in alchemy, we spend our lives seeking gold, which may be hidden by lead. In our everyday life is where we can find something precious, we can find elements of meaning.

As young people we all want to be beautiful or handsome for a multitude of reasons. As we age and our perception of beauty changes, we don't lose the desire to be beautiful, but it undergoes a massive change. I remember vividly walking through a restaurant at the same time as an eighteen-year-old and all heads turned to observe her as she walked to her table. I was a little behind her, so I could see all the men looking at her. She had the beauty and confidence of youth and I, in my forties, realized that I was no longer eye-catching.

But we get looks when we are old, too. A beautiful friend confessed that far more people have told her that she was attractive in her late years, as opposed to when she was young. People admire an older man or woman who has retained mystery or aliveness. It's not about physical beauty anymore. It's about the beauty of experience, of having been through something that has etched the experience into our faces. I saw a daytime TV talk show host on a program recently and audibly gasped at seeing her face. She was in her late sixties or early seventies and she'd had bad plastic surgery done and looked horrible. Her face wore a mask-like expression, pasty skin, and bulging lips. No one could have said that she allowed us even a little peek at her soul. It was there somewhere, but no longer visible. She had always been kind of tough as an interviewer, but now she looked frightening.

When we are old our skin becomes more transparent, and so must we. The thickness of our persona has to give way. The ego has to go to the college of experience and learn a whole new way of being. When that happens, you will feel more beautiful or handsome. An old friend stunned me when she said, "I went right from being a teenager into old age. I skipped middle age completely, so you can imagine what a shock it was to realize I was old."

The first indication of being old doesn't come from a mirror, it comes from the people who bag your groceries and remark how young you look, thinking that they are giving you a desired compliment. But often they don't mean you LOOK young, they mean you don't seem OLD. It is your life force, or lack of it, that catches their attention. We need to take a sense of energy on our journey into old age—not necessarily physical energy, but an energy directed toward life, either inner or outer. Ageless people, whether ill or not, have an energy and enthusiasm for life that emanates an aura of vitality and youth. In the introvert that energy is seen when a deep passion for a book or piece of artwork is shared. In an extravert the energy may express through a fascination with the world and sharing his or her experience of it.

The second indication we have of aging is indeed the mirror. Whenever I have gone through terrible times, my face always shows the pain of grief and fear I am experiencing. And when I see THAT face, I feel that I will probably look like this forever. I think that is a very human trait. The suffering that the soul experiences leaves a stamp upon our faces.

And the last indication of age has to do with slowing down and the recognition that what we used to do in 10 minutes now takes a half hour. That the perception of time has changed appreciably is often our first awareness that we are no longer the master of our own choices.

Consider the story of Lot's wife, who was turned into a pillar of salt as a punishment for not obeying Yahweh's order not to look back upon Sodom and Gomorrah while fleeing. In spite of the warning, she just couldn't resist looking back. We've all seen individuals who have spent their entire life in the past, not seeing the present or future possibilities, but only what once was. Salt is a very good symbol for bitterness because it is indeed a bitter mineral. In small amounts it adds zest to food, but drop a cup of it into a tasty dish and there is no way to retrieve the dish's original flavor. In other words, too much bitterness spoils the flavor of life.

A friend's mother spent her life looking to the past, regretting that she didn't marry the handsome young poet with whom she was in love at 18. Her parents forbade her to marry him, and she didn't run away with him. Instead, she stayed at home taking care of her parents, not becoming the concert pianist she dreamed of being, marrying at a much later age, and giving birth to two children. Both children were remarkable and intelligent and very attractive, but she never really saw them; her gaze was always upon the past. She didn't see the man she married either, and eventually they parted. And finally in her old age, while I was visiting, she happened to tell me a dream she'd had repeatedly throughout her life, and in that dream she was running to catch a bus. She could see the bus at the stop, but just as she arrived, the bus pulled away from the curb without her. Every night, for forty years, she'd had this dream, never realizing that the dream might have been saying, "Stop spending so much time looking back because as long as you do, you will be too late to catch the bus into life."

Many women and men have that same attitude toward aging. They look back to their youthful bodies, their young self, and regret aging and all that goes with it. And if we do that, in some ways we do not get on the bus that takes us into this phase of life.

The worst part of the previous story is that the woman didn't recognize the amazing achievement of giving birth to these two souls who were special and talented children that any mother would be proud to call son and daughter. Instead she focused on what she didn't have and died an embittered woman at a very old age.

Salt. Bitterness attends all grief and loss as a possibility. At one time or another it is human to feel the taste of bitterness in our mouth, but as a steady diet it will kill us. We can look at our old faces and bodies and breasts or chests and recognize that we are not the same in any way. Everything has sagged and let go, and gravity is winning every battle. But what else is happening at the same time? What, indeed.

When midlife arrives, we begin to be aware of lines creeping into out brow and around our eyes. "Crow's feet" they call them, and they do look like a crow has stamped upon the fresh, taut skin of youth and caused this imprint, this scar that cannot be removed except by extreme measures and pain.

Around midlife, and despite the crow's feet, a surge of creativity is often felt. We take classes, go back to school, get degrees in whatever has been aborted by marriage or having to work. We study, take responsibility for our minds and thinking (which Jung wrote is especially good for women), and often as we sculpt or paint we begin to take ourselves more seriously.

In old age things get even more interesting. A big transformation occurs in many of us. We stop being interested in pleasing people. Wow, what a change and relief that is! And along with that we no longer care what people think. I mean, we REALLY don't care what people think and make it known to one and all. In women the animus gets stronger, and we are able to cut through things that used to be daunting and, in fact, like how that feels. It isn't that we become "animusy," it's that we find ourselves with something to say, and we step out and say it. As Betty Meador recently said, "We older women have a lot to say." And so do men. They often experience a development of the anima and find themselves experiencing life from a different perspective.

When wrinkles cover our faces and our breasts and stomachs sag, we have become the individual we have always dreamed we'd be one day. This is what I think it means when a woman is compared to a beautiful rose. The stem and thorns represent the path during the early years, childhood and adolescence and later, when life is full of problems and thorns. Falling in love and falling out of love. Finding a mate or being found by one and getting married—each experience carries its own thorn. Each thorn represents a setback or a missed opportunity or a trial physically or mentally. Then as a girl becomes a woman she meets the full, rich, fragrant head of the rose and the silky smoothness of the petals and the realization of beauty. First thorns and then the beauty. Then at the end of life, the petals loosen and let go, fluttering to the ground.

Or, like the magazine ad I found in a doctor's office: a picture of a bucket of coal out of a mine and a picture of a faceted diamond. The heading under the coal read "Before aging"; under the diamond it read, "After aging."

Being truly beautiful comes after a lifetime of experience. There is, of course, beauty to youth and innocence. No varicosity, no aching bones in youth, only the possibility of everything going one's way. But with old age comes certitude and a lack of concern for what others think that creates a softness and ease in meeting life. There is also a comfort knowing that in old age we have the daily awareness of how close we are to death. One has only to read the obituary pages. In the acceptance of the reality of death and the reconciliation of living and dying, which is the real work of being old, comes a serenity that is palpable.

Another quality we need to take with us on this journey is a sense of fullness. Getting old becomes a series of things one gives up. It starts innocently enough with simple pleasures, such as coffee or chocolate, or the fact that we need to rest more and can't go out as much, or we give up wearing high heels and panty hose, or our waist thickens—all varieties of giving up. But as we relinquish some things, we may gain other valuable gems; for example, our curiosity about life and death. We need our curiosity to stay very much alive. We need it so we can dare to try new things about which we are curious. We need it so we can allow the inner child free reign from time to time so we can retain that ageless quality we cherish. And we need it to keep us learning, alert, and alive.

I think women of ideas and passion are beautiful women, such as the late Dr. Marie-Louse von Franz, author and analyst, who attracted the love and loyalty of many men and women. I was in my twenties when we met, she in her thirties. She was beautiful then, and her beauty grew as she aged in spite of a devastating illness. She planned her own funeral, and it was a celebration of life with food, classical music, and joy.

Other examples of beautiful women who were not born beautiful are Eleanor Roosevelt, a woman known around the world, and Dr. Rivkah Scharf Kluger, known only in her circle as a scholar in ancient Middle Eastern history and mythology, particularly having to do with Judaic and Sumerian religions. Eleanor Roosevelt was not only not a beauty by societal standards, she was considered downright unattractive. Rivkah Scharf didn't marry Yeheskal Kluger until she was mature. So impassioned was she about her work that when she lectured on the Gilgamesh Epic, it was as if a light shone from within her and radiated into and around the room. I saw her at one of the first lectures she gave in Los Angeles in the 1950s and thought her to be utterly beautiful. When I saw her at another event where she was a dinner guest, I was amazed to see how ordinary her appearance was: she was a smallish, round woman with forward-leaning posture, warm and lively brown eyes, and a lot of personal charm, but far from beautiful. It was her work on the Old Testament that made her beautiful, because that was her passion.

Eleanor Roosevelt has been a favorite public figure since I was a child. I thought her uniqueness and kindness were good examples to follow. What these women have in common is that they had a passion, to which they were willing to devote their lives. Passion for an idea or belief is one of the ingredients in being beautiful while old.

I will close with this excerpt from a letter written by C.G. Jung and quoted in Marie-Louise von Franz's *On Dreams and Death*. His words provide a new way of thinking about the end of our last journey:

> This spectacle of old age would be unendurable did we not know that our psyche reaches into a region held captive neither by change in time nor by limitation of place. In that form of being our birth is a death and our death a birth. The scales of the whole hang balanced.[112]

---

112 von Franz, *Dreams and Death*, 155.

Chapter 16

BODY AND SOUL

Originally published in *Psychological Perspectives*[113]

Standing in line at the grocery checkout counter, I gaze at the rack of magazines. My attention is captured by a magazine with bold headings that read: BODY + SOUL. Not body *and* soul, body *plus* soul. The notion of synchronicity went through my thoughts as I bought *InStyle,* a magazine dedicated to BEAUTY + LIFESTYLE + FASHION + CELEBRITY. After putting the groceries away and curling up on the couch to read, I found it a revelation. For the most part (no surprise here) the articles instructed women in the art of shaping up and saving their skin and shared fitness secrets of the stars. Yet the theme of "body + soul" was included, and deeper issues were addressed.

InStyle highlighted the relation of body to soul by giving its readers a thoughtful piece of photojournalism about a young woman who is a popular singer as well as a committed athlete who competes as a triathlete. Reading the article, I was very moved by the depth of commitment the singer expressed both to her body and to her music. Like many who espouse open-mindedness, my snobbish attitude about the popular culture came clattering to the floor, badly dented, as I found the ideas to be fresh and creative without being "psychological." I liked it.

Our bodies and souls are inextricably linked. There is no body without soul and no soul without body . . . or it feels that we cannot perceive of this. When we become depressed in our soul, we experience what shamans call *loss of soul,* which can involve feelings of dullness, illness,

---

113   Gilda Frantz, "Body and Soul," *Psychological Perspectives* 42(1), (2001): 8-11.

emptiness, and meaninglessness, and can be the cause of great suffering. According to shamanic teachings we can become ill when our animal spirits leave, or when we suffer loss of soul. This occurs when the spirit or soul is neglected, bored, or is wounded in some way. Shamanic belief that the soul must be retrieved in order for the person to feel whole again is at the heart of the sacred practices.

Although they don't usually phrase it that way, many individuals often come into analysis for soul retrieval. During such a time, the body may or may not continue to function, but they feel dead spiritually. Being ill does not always indicate a loss of soul, but it can. Being physically paralyzed doesn't mean loss of soul, in fact quite the contrary. Often when the body is very ill, there can be an experience of the fullness of the soul. What a mystery!

I have been present when death has occurred and have "seen" the flight of the soul when the body stops breathing and the heart ceases to beat. When life leaves the body, the soul seems to float freely, going wherever souls go. When we experience a transcendent spiritual experience, we often feel it in the body. Mystics have used the language of sexuality (body) to describe such experiences, and individuals who revere the body often speak of having had a mystical experience during a physical feat of strength or endurance.

At what feels like a very late age, I have begun to become more aware of my body, like many older people seem to be doing today. I have begun to learn to exercise and to understand that care of the soul is also care of the body. After years of seemingly ignoring the body, I have become a kind of "senior jock" who never wants to miss a session of exercise and never misses a chance to show off the results of my strength training.

We often think that focusing utterly on the soul will be the salvation of everything, as if the soul were not in the body as well. It takes half our lifetime to understand the body and the other half learning to give the body what it needs. The same could be said about the soul.

Chapter 17

JUNG, AGING, AND INDIVIDUATION

Originally published in *Psychological Perspectives*[114]

Recently, unbidden, a magazine came through the mail slot along with the mail. It had the curious name of *More* and had my name and address on the front, although I never have subscribed to this publication. I quickly leafed through it, and the title of an article that had to do with aging caught my eye. I looked at the cover again and noted that the entire magazine had as its theme the experience of getting older.

I find this interest in aging curious. I am old already, so I don't have that sense of shock and surprise that comes when one is 50 and begins to notice a wrinkle here or that one cannot suck in her belly. And I am speaking from a woman's point of view. I noticed that all the articles in the magazine about aging were addressed to women. There were no photos of old or older men with skinny calves and overhanging bellies. I am certain men pay attention to getting older and that it strikes a similar note of vanity in men as it does in women. I think that men simply are not the focus of multimillion dollar businesses to help them stay young—you know, those pricey face creams that tighten and makes one's skin feel silky.

Some years ago I wrote a paper on aging which I titled "Agelessness: The Very Soul of Beauty."[115] It is a pretty upbeat paper, seen from the

---

114 Gilda Frantz, "Jung, Aging, and Individuation," *Psychological Perspectives* 56(2), (2013): 129-132.

115 Gilda Frantz, "Being Ageless: The Very Soul of Beauty," *Psychological Perspectives* 50(1), (2007): 31-51.

eyes of a woman who is just eighty. At eighty, I found, a woman can still be upbeat and find it within herself to take a positive view of all the changes that have taken place, both inside of her and outside of her. Now I am six years older and have a slightly different perspective. I still see that getting old is a kind of adventure that ends at the end of a tunnel, but there have been certain events that have made me enlarge my views quite a bit.

Halfway through my eightieth year I experienced a huge loss that made me feel crushed, and I became physically ill. I didn't have anything life-threatening, but I was incapacitated by the loss and stopped driving or reading or doing much of anything. I had developed vestibular labyrinth neuritis in my inner ear, which caused a kind of dizziness that made life unbearable. It could strike any time, day or night, and since I lived alone it was very hard to function, given that I couldn't walk or see anything clearly when dizzy. I was treated by a fine neurologist, but the condition became chronic and lasted for years.

I would sit in a comfortable chair for hours either getting over a dizzy spell or simply thinking. Reading hurt my eyes, as did watching television, so both were out of the question. While visiting an old friend, I had seen very old people in nursing homes who sat and stared into space, and I would wonder if that is what I was doing. Every shred of my positive attitude toward getting old seemed to vanish as I struggled to maintain both my balance and my perspective. Not having balance was the most difficult in many ways.

I finally did what my beloved daughter suggested when she saw the pain I was in, and began Jungian analysis again with a much younger analyst. It was just what I needed. I began to use my imagination and to feel excited about writing. I did active imagination with inner figures and felt something that had been rigid and stagnant begin to move within myself. I renewed my commitment to writing my thoughts in my dream journal, and I began to feel better. The dizziness didn't just stop immediately, but in my heart and soul I had begun to regain my center. I had a nurse around the clock and still needed her, but I could see that one day I would regain my independence, which filled my heart with cheer.

But the whole process really took longer than I would have imagined, and even now I have nurse's aide who stays with me at night. The profound loss of balance and independence shoved me to the ground, humbled me, and gave me a different perspective on old age. Although I was widowed young, in my late 40s, I could now imagine how shattering it is to be old and lose one's mate. After a lifetime of living side by side, it must be devastating to find that life's exegesis must be met alone. I began to take walks again, but with much less confidence than I'd had before the dizziness. *Confidence.* This was a loss to me when I learned that it had abandoned me as a steady part of my existence. Falling became a frightening reality, and I still walk very slowly to be sure my steps are firm and steady. My balance has never come back as it used to be.

All of this is by way of saying that if an old person is ailing, there is a feeling of depletion and vulnerability in making one's way in the world. I didn't drive a car during the time that I was dizzy. When I finally stabilized, three or four years had passed. I looked at the odometer on my 2007 car and saw that I had driven very few miles in the years since I purchased it. Even now, in 2013, I have put very few miles on it in the six years I've owned the car. I no longer drive on freeways or at night. Having been an excellent driver with an excellent record, I realized that my reflexes didn't work as rapidly as they did when I was younger. One day in the near future, I will give up driving altogether.

I think it was wise to do what I did, but each time I gave something up, I found I had less of a sense of being at the helm. And I wasn't. That is the whole point to aging, to realize that it is not MY way but THY way. I don't say I am going to do this or that, I say I will do it if I am PERMITTED. It is an entirely different way to live.

As I have previously mentioned, in old age we have to live in relation to the Self, not to the ego as we did as a young person, and I believe that this is even more true when we are old and ill. The body does extract a kind of humbleness on the part of each of us in old age because some of us are limited physically, and there is no getting around being slow because of it.

Perspective. If you are reading this and are old, don't forget to try to recapture your perspective on the way to recovering your health. It is from having a perspective that is humble and understands that life as an old person is lived day to day, that we can continue to enjoy life. I love life. I love the smell of the earth and the flowers of the fields. All of this is part of my perspective on life and keeps me sane and steady. Oh, I falter from time to time. We all do, but it's how we recover that makes the difference.

Part 6

OUR JUNGIAN ANCESTORS

The development of personality from the germ-state to full consciousness is at once a charisma and a curse, because its first fruit is the conscious and unavoidable segregation of the single individual from the undifferentiated and unconscious herd. This means isolation, and there is no more comforting word for it. Neither family nor society nor position can save him from this fate, nor yet the most successful adaptation to his environment, however smoothly he fits in. The development of personality is a favour that must be paid for dearly.

—C.G. Jung[116]

---

116 C.G. Jung, "The Development of the Personality," CW 17, ¶ 294.

Chapter 18

I'LL SEE YOU IN MY DREAMS

Originally Presented at the National Conference
of Jungian Analysts[117]

In 1950, when I married my husband, Kieffer Frantz, I also married into the Jungian community in Los Angeles. For the most part, they were a sober, intensely introverted and dedicated group. The Jungian circle was a small one, both locally and worldwide. There may have been between 100 and 200 analysts in the entire world in 1950. At that time, as now, there were centers in San Francisco, New York, and Los Angeles (which was the last one formed). James Kirsch was the only analyst in Los Angeles who could certify individuals to become analysts. There was less than a handful of people who had that aspiration, my husband among them. One needs to remember that it wasn't until 1953 and 1954 that Volumes 7, 12, 16, and 17 of Jung's papers were published in America. To fill this void, James Kirsch translated *Answer to Job* after it was published in Europe in 1952 and made copies of his translation for his students. My husband often ordered Jung's books from England—for example, *Psychological Types, Modern Man in Search of a Soul,* and *Essays on Contemporary Events.*

I think the reason that Los Angeles is often associated with what is now called the "classical school of Jungian psychology" involved two factors. One was James and Hilde's desire to stay close to Zürich in spirit and thought. The other factor was the resourceful manner in which they

---

117   Gilda Frantz, "I'll See You in My Dreams." (paper presented at the National Conference of Jungian Analysts, Lake Tahoe, Nevada, October 1994).

dealt with the issue of *how* to "stay close." Within the Analytical Psychology Club, which they founded (along with Max and Lore Zeller and
others), they created an education fund for the express purpose of bringing Zürich analysts to Los Angeles. Many analysts and their analysands
contributed money to this fund. In 1952 Rivkah Scharf Kluger was the
first Swiss analyst to come. She was treated a little like royalty (as were
all the speakers), and she brought a unique kind of scholarship that provided us with stimulating new ideas. Rivkah specialized in Gilgamesh
and the Old Testament, and she made the myth come alive. In the early
fifties, *every* topic was new to most of us.

Marie-Louise von Franz followed with Barbara Hannah. Marie-Louise, who was around 38 at that time, was utterly natural and unpreten-
tious. I recall that she told me she had recently completed her first book
on fairy tales, which was done in collaboration with another person.
That individual, without von Franz's knowledge, had taken von Franz's
name off the book and had it published under only the collaborator's
name. At the time of her visit to Los Angeles, this experience was still
painfully fresh; she was extremely hurt by the betrayal, which involved
her life's work. I also recall that, as a part of her trip to our country, she
was going to go horseback riding in Montana or Wyoming, because she
had always wanted to do this. I think she was fascinated by the Wild
West. I loaned her a pair of blue jeans so that she could ride comfortably.

Esther Harding, Eleanor Bertine, and C.A. Meier came too, as did
many others. After hearing the lectures, we would stand around talking
in the rented hall, and then still feeling excited, we would go for coffee
and talk into the night, arguing pro and con ideas about what we had
heard. Then when we got home, we wouldn't be able to sleep, we'd be
so stirred up. Jung's depth psychology made us feel completely *awake*.

We also exchanged gossip about each other and our analysts. This
gossip was our way of humanizing the analytic situation so that it didn't
become too "thick and rich." As a tiny band of true believers (I now
included myself), we were electrified by all these new thoughts and possibilities. Analysts, analysands, and trainees all attended the lectures.
We had receptions for the speakers and we made a fuss over them. A
lecture was always an event. Today we analysts rarely go to lectures, in

Los Angeles anyway. I rarely go myself. Whereas once the Analytical Psychology Club was comprised of both analysts and non-analysts, now the meetings are almost exclusively attended by non-analysts.

James and Hilde Kirsch were influenced by Zürich in their work, and they attempted to give their analysands an experience of what it was like to have worked in Zürich. They may have erred on the side of becoming too friendly with some of their analysands, but they brought these individuals what they themselves had experienced. What had the Kirsches found in Jung? Was it a new light, something that shone so brightly that it illuminated corners of their inner selves in ways that were startling and incredible? Was it working with the Self? Or was it knowing something about the shadow? I think it was the latter, because the individuals who began the Los Angeles group had all experienced true evil during their lifetimes: They all came from Germany, and they were all Jewish.

The Kirsches were not at all sentimental about Jung, the man. If you have seen the film *Matter of Heart*, that seems to be true of most of his followers. Although they respected him greatly, they, unlike many people today, were able to separate the man from his work. The day after Jung died in 1961, I said to Hilde Kirsch, "Aren't you sad? What do you think will happen in the Jungian world now that Jung is gone?" Her reply was very much like her. She said, "Well, now, I suppose people will be able to accomplish what they were not able to do when Jung was alive." Upon reflection, she probably was talking about male analysts who felt obscured by Jung's genius.

The unique combination of depth psychology and hospitality has left its brand on many of us in the Los Angeles group. Hilde and James Kirsch and later, Max and Lore Zeller, provided hospitable centers in their homes for all Jungians who passed through Los Angeles. By opening their homes to us, they held our group together, before we had our own building. For around 45 years the Kirsches gave seminars in their home! These seminars would go on for years, as each of them went into great depth in imparting Jung's work. That particular kind of European scholarship was part of their culture and education. I think we have seen the last of such patience and willingness to devote that kind of time. It was a rare experience to attend those seminars.

My analyst was a very quiet person. She would often comment to me, "The unconscious doesn't like that," or "The unconscious wants you to do such-and-such." I listened and found a way to relate to the unconscious on a daily basis, because I trusted her. In Los Angeles we were encouraged to do active imagination, to write, draw, and sculpt our dreams in clay as though it were a matter of life and death. The *urgent* need for consciousness was, I believe, a special legacy of our founders in Los Angeles.

One of the issues I worked on in analysis was my concern that my child was "different" and that I was doing something "wrong." According to the climate of that time, it seemed clear that I was responsible for my son being different, and like a lot of women, I was only too willing to accept society's—as well as my analyst's—authority on that point. So I struggled with the Great Mother and *Puer* archetypes. Recent research on the origins of homosexuality indicate that my self-reproach was not founded in reality—in other words, it may not have been "my fault." Still, I found the analytical work extremely honest and transformative. I became very well acquainted with the Great Mother archetype, and active imagination became a way of contacting the truths that resided within my psyche.

Unfortunately, in the mid-1950s no one knew very much about homosexuality, including Jung (and it is still not too well understood by some analysts). Many years later, when my son "came out," Hilde Kirsch asked me if I was angry with her. I told her I wasn't angry, and still am not today, because I know we were *all* working in the dark then. In the 1950s the light of consciousness only shined so far. In my life, Jung's discoveries freed me from suffering in one way, yet subjected me to suffering in another. I think this is always the case with new discoveries: There is always the combined elements of healing *and* injury.

I recall visiting Sequoia National Park with Kieffer many years ago. A park ranger took a group of us into Crystal Cavern. We entered the artificially lit cave and were immediately awed by its vast size and the huge stalagmites and stalactites (but I still don't know which point down and which point up). After giving us a lecture on the cavern, the park ranger turned off the artificial light so that we could experience total darkness. He wanted to show us what early humans faced when coming into such a cave seeking shelter. When the light was turned off, I stood stock still in utter, impenetrable darkness. I literally could not see my own hand in front of my face. Then the ranger struck a match and lit a small candle. I will never forget that *one candle's ability* to illuminate the entire cavern, to lift the darkness that enveloped us. In my life, Jung's work lit the candle.

We are living in a dark time, in an age of fear. In a letter written almost 40 years ago, Jung wrote:

> Noise is certainly only one of the evils of our time . . . the alarming pollution of our water supplies, the steady increase of radioactivity, and the somber threat of overpopulation with its genocidal tendencies have already led to a widespread though not generally conscious *fear* which loves noise because it stops the fear from being heard. *Noise is welcome because it drowns out the inner instinctive warning.* Fear seeks noisy company and pandemonium to scare away the demons. . . . The dark side of the picture is that we wouldn't have noise if we didn't secretly want it. . . If there were silence, their fear would make people reflect, and there is no knowing what might then come to consciousness.[118]

I fear that consciousness is in danger of becoming lost once again, in danger of slipping into the quicksand of the unconscious marsh. At the end of his life Jung said that he guarded his consciousness, lest it be taken from him. I recall thinking, "How could that be? How could one's consciousness be *taken* away?" Later I realized that perhaps Jung was acknowledging that we are always vulnerable to becoming unconsciously identified with the collective, to failing to hold the tension of the opposites within, to forgetting to seek out and relate to that within which is true and constant. There are many ways we can lose what has been gained in a lifetime.

These are dangerous times. The opposites are getting increasingly polarized. The split between those who *have* and those who *have not* is

---

118 C.G. Jung, *Letters*, Vol. 2, ¶¶ 389-390.

greater than ever. World economic conditions are continually unstable. In 1946 Jung wrote the following words, which I feel apply today:

> We are living in time of great disruption: political passions are aflame, internal upheavals have brought nations to the brink of chaos. . . .This critical state of things has such a tremendous influence on the psychic life of the individual *that the doctor must follow its effects with more than usual attention.* . . . He feels the violence . . . even in the quiet of his consulting room. . . . He [the analyst] cannot afford to withdraw to the *peaceful island of undisturbed scientific work,* but must constantly descend into the arena of world events, in order to join in the battle of conflicting passions and opinions. Were he to remain aloof from the tumult, the calamity of our time would reach him only from afar, and his patients' suffering would find neither ear nor understanding. . . . For this reason he cannot avoid coming to grips with contemporary history, even if his very soul shrinks from the . . . uproar . . . propaganda . . . and the jarring speeches.[119]

The ingredients of poverty, hopelessness, and fear may be all that are needed to create a revolution or a war or another Hitler. The need has never been so great as it is now for individuals to *stay centered.* I know that many of us are exhausted. Is it because we are trying to live a more collective life as opposed to paying heed to the inner world? We all need to listen carefully so that we do not get engulfed or overwhelmed by the collective tide. We need to get very quiet so that we can hear the deep rumblings within the psyche of the world.

Where did the energy come from in the early days of Jungian psychology? The founders worked long hours in their analytic work with patients, gave frequent seminars, dealt with everyday family issues and the tasks of making a living and raising their children. What is the origin of their sense of destiny and mission? Clearly the Los Angeles group was deeply influenced by Hilde and James Kirsch's and Max Zeller's experiences in Nazi Germany. Although Max rarely spoke about his

---

119 C.G. Jung, Preface to "Essays on Contemporary Events," CW 10, ¶ 177, emphasis added.

time in the concentration camp, the experience profoundly informed his life. It has been said that Los Angeles developed a "refugee mentality" because our founders were all Jewish refugees. While it is true that they were refugees, I don't think that theory quite fits. I believe we, as a new group, became deeply connected to the unconscious, and all that implies, because our founders had looked evil in the face; they had learned about evil in the most direct way imaginable.

All had been born and raised in Germany, had enjoyed life there. Hilde Kirsch's ancestors could be traced back 900 years in Berlin, which is very unusual for a Jew. That span of centuries implies that Hilde's family lived safe and secure lives there. When Hitler sounded his war cry, Hilde and James and Max saw and felt the psychic infection at close range, suffering deeply as a result of that infection. They had been part of the Holocaust.

I believe that whenever Hilde or James or Max spoke about becoming overly identified with the collective or about the importance of developing a relationship to the unconscious, their point of reference was what had transpired in Nazi Germany as much as what went on in Zürich. Because of their experiences, they were deeply committed to the reality of the psyche, and everything in their life underscored that commitment. As I said, doing active imagination, working with dreams, was more a life-or-death undertaking than merely good analytic behavior.

Jung's early followers had a sense of social responsibility; they were cognizant of their role in bringing forth what Jung wrote into the world. I think this was true for all the early founders of Jungian centers. Every institute in this country was begun by analysts who were trained or analyzed in Zürich.

I am sure that each of these centers have much in common with one another, but the Los Angeles center was begun by analysts who had experienced the evil of fascism firsthand and knew how dangerous it was for evil to be allowed to remain unconscious.

In the early days here in Los Angeles there was a sense of wonder, without being worshipful. I remember my late husband saying that he did not want to create another church. I ask again, where did this sense of destiny come from? True, they had worked with C.G. himself—that must have opened their eyes. They had experienced the Self in its light and dark aspects, and they had seen true evil and knew of its existence in the collective as well as within each person. We in Los Angeles were the recipients of this knowledge and it was conveyed to us in clear, straight-forward terms. They didn't say, "Jung said this," or "Jung said that." It was *their experience of Jung* that was passed on to us by their living relationship to the unconscious. The unconscious was not a place out in the ocean or in the heavens somewhere: The objective psyche was a *living* reality.

Like most people who have been immersed in the Jungian community, I have had dreams of analysts such as Esther Harding, Barbara Hannah, and Marie-Louise von Franz. When I was in Zürich many years ago, I met Barbara Hannah at a conference and I said, "Oh, Miss Hannah, I had a dream about you last night" (she didn't even know me), and she responded in her thick British accent, "Ah, yes, one *does* get around in dreams," and we laughed. As a young married woman, I had a dream about Jung that played a pivotal role in my life. Before I report this dream, however, a little background about the dreamer is necessary.

When I was a young child I lived in Santa Monica, not far from where I live today. This was the 1930s and we were feeling the effects of the Depression, as was everyone. There was a pervasive sense of desperation and defeat that became all too familiar. My mother found comfort by consulting psychics, reading her horoscope, and sometimes attending seances. My mother, sister, and I told our dreams at breakfast, and my mother would interpret them. What she said was more like village superstition than dream analysis, but it left me with a lifelong interest in dreams and the mantic arts. My sister's husband read mystical books and spoke of karma and fate. I had always thought I had had a terrible childhood, until one day I realized that mine was the childhood of an individual who was being prepared to work with the unconscious. Later, my marriage to Kieffer and my introduction to Jungian psychology utterly changed my life. Our two children and my marriage were the most important influences on my life.

When I had this dream, I was neither an analyst nor in the training program. I had been in analysis for a length of time and still possessed a carefully hidden but real sense of inferiority. When the time came to enter the training program, remembering this dream gave me courage.

Jung was sitting on a bench in the woods, near Bollingen, and he was very old. (In real life he was dead.) I was seated next to him. He took off his ring and said, "I want you to have this ring because you are going to take care of me." He gave me his ring.

As was her nature, my analyst said very little, but it was clear to us both that it was a special dream, unlike any I had ever had. Looking back, I feel that I needed to have an experience of Jung *within my own psyche*. To me, Jung is the carrier of consciousness in our time. I needed that dream. He might have said, "Take care of my work, take care of my legacy." I recall von Franz's first meeting with Jung, when he told her of a woman who had dreamed she was on the moon. von Franz had said, "But that was a dream." Jung's reply has always stayed with me. He said, "She *was* on the moon." That is how I understood my dream—as an absolute reality.

Rings have always had a special meaning to me from the time I was given a little ring as a child and lost it. I was in the first grade. With the gift came the warning: Never take this ring off or you will lose it. I treasured it because it had a colored stone. I wore it to school and a friend asked to try it on and, ignoring the warning, I gave it to her. When she took the ring off her finger, she placed it on my lunch tray. When the bell rang, forgetting my ring, I tossed the contents of the tray into the trash barrel and went off to class. It wasn't until school was over that I remembered my ring. By then, the trash had gone out and, with it, my ring.

In my reading, I discovered that the first ring was worn by Prometheus as a symbolic remnant of his chains. Rings also symbolize eternity, which is why they are exchanged along with marriage vows in many cultures. I have always been fascinated by the ring Jung wore, which depicted a snake. Giving me this ring meant that the gift I was given was his work. I have tried to be true to that dream. I am only one of many individuals who feel deeply about Jung's work—that it needs to be cared for and nurtured. Individuals have used his research as a springboard for their own ideas. I've read some authors who believe they have exceeded his scope and his reach. What matters is that we judge the man on his work and not on whether he lived his life in a certain way. He was, after all, a man of his own time, a man with flaws, no matter how visionary his ideas. But he was always true to himself and we should do no less.

I have always liked Jung's proposition that the problems of life are never fully solved; that it is how we try to *relate* to the problems that makes life interesting.

Recently I came upon a first-person account of an actual meeting with Jung in the book, *C.G. Jung, Emma Jung, and Toni Wolff: A Collection of Remembrances*. Mary Louise Ainsworth is speaking:

> He [Jung] first spoke of Africa and the conflict between primitive and civilized man. Then, as we began a discussion of the serpent symbol, *Dr. Jung handed me his well-worn black ring, that was the Agathos Daimon, the crowned cobra, that he always wore, and I turned it around in my hands as he went on talking.*

He went on to explain:

> "We cannot kill the serpent, that defenseless animal. We must have him near, for two reasons: one, that his poison may be an antidote so we are not caught unawares by his sting—then we are protected. We must see that he is not loose in the world. By bearing the opposites, we can expose ourselves to life in our humanity. Otherwise he may kill us. We have to realize the evil is in us: we have to risk life, to get into life, then it takes on color; otherwise we might as well read a book. Satan is a snake." He added, "Christ is too." [120]

Writing in his journal in 1990 after he knew he was HIV-positive, my son wrote the following observations about evil:

> This epidemic will ultimately inspire works of great beauty and power. It is an irony of life. Some of the greatest creative works of man have been born out of pain and suffering. So what is evil, in that case? We think of the epidemic as a

---

120   *C.G. Jung, Emma Jung, and Toni Wolff: A Collection of Remembrances*, 111, emphasis added.

bad thing and I, for one, am not exactly jumping for joy at the thought of my oh-so-likely to be foreshortened life. . . . And yet, when I think of what the gift to the future will be from this . . . the art, the dance, the theater, literature, and music that will derive not so much from the "global" kind of response to the disaster that is AIDS, but from the personal loss, I have to wonder.

Maybe what is evil is not necessarily what causes suffering, but suffering without some kind of gain, either in insight, depth of being, or creative expression. The idea is hard to express precisely. . . . Maybe it is the response that is the key . . . that there is an evil response to suffering. A destructive response.

I heard it said recently that people don't dream about Jung anymore. How could that be? Is it that our patients do not dream about Jung because we are no longer connected to what Jung stands for? That we are not passing on to our analysands the fire and light of consciousness? If that is true, then Jung will indeed be lost and will have to be rediscovered in the future (Edward Edinger, private conversation).

I think we should take care of Jung's work by being true to each other. Some analysts have gone outside the Jungian community for analytical work for a number of reasons. Seeking such outside help goes back a long way in our history. If their experience of Jungian psychology felt inadequate, it must be remembered that there are still those of us who remain satisfied with our Jungian analytical and theoretical experiences. There is nothing wrong with "doing one's own thing"—we all do our thing, one way or another. But when another analytical discipline is united with Jungian psychology, that doesn't make it Jungian. And those of us who follow Jung's path should try to understand that there are those who need to go outside their Jungian work for one reason or another.

In my own analysis I don't think I ever got an answer to very much, if anything. *But I was encouraged to discover and pursue my own truth.* We are living in a dangerous age. It will take a miracle to get us out of the troubles we humans have created. The publication of *The Celestine Prophecy*, with its huge popularity, indicates to me that people want to experience the numinous. Iron curtains have fallen or have been taken down, people are trying not to harm the earth and atmosphere. But so much hate and violence remain in the world that we all must be as conscious as possible, to hold the center within ourselves, so that the world can recover a center one day as well.

Chapter 19

SPIRITUAL JOURNEYS

Originally published in *Psychological Perspectives*[121]

In the past year I have been on sabbatical. It was an opportunity to reflect upon thoughts that encroached as my years multiply. It was a good year to read and write, and now I am back and ready to be part of the outer world again.

In October of 2009, *The Red Book* was published after being locked away in a vault for many years. A fascinating series of events brought this about. Even finding the publisher was a synchronistic experience. The publisher decided to release a first printing of 5,000 copies. I have a feeling that the thinking was, after all, this book is $195, and we are having difficult economic times, so let's be conservative. The books flew out of bookstores before they were on the shelves, and by now I think W. W. Norton has printed 25,000 copies and counting.

I went to New York for the grand party that accompanied *The Red Book's* publication date. It was held at the Rubin Museum, where the original *Red Book* was displayed for all to see. It has been on exhibit in New York for five months and is now in Los Angeles at the Hammer Museum. For those of you who have not yet seen *The Red Book*, it is a complete facsimile of the calligraphy and paintings of Jung's spiritual journey from 1915 to 1930. There is nothing quite like this book. Run to your nearest bookseller and get a copy.

---

121 Gilda Frantz, "Spiritual Journeys," *Psychological Perspectives* 53(2), (2010): 131-132.

While at the gala opening a friend suggested that some of us might like to read *The Red Book* together, and we now meet twice a month at my home and read the book aloud for two hours. We discuss it, cry a little, hold our hearts and gasp. It is a phenomenal revelation of an individuation journey and the ordeal of the reconciliation of the opposites within.

Sitting in my office in a cozy leather chair, now alone, I close *The Red Book* and remain in a kind of reverie. I've cried while reading it and my heart feels cracked open. I have always gotten so much out of reading Jung's books, but this exquisite writing has a voice that feels things I know about. Jung has always felt very human to me, and now more so in *The Red Book*. I thank God daily for being able to read it, that I didn't die before it was published. I thank the Jung family for permitting the publication of this seminal book against their protective stance toward their grandfather and his creative work. I include in my prayers the two men who joined forces to bring this book to light: one, the scholar (Sonu Shamdasani) who spent 13 years (at least) translating and reading these rich and dense pages; the other (Steve Martin) the Jungian analyst and visionary who knew he could go out into the world and simply by telling people about Jung and *The Red Book*, and about the scholar's work, could inspire people to make major contributions that would bring this treasure out of a vault into the light of day. My heart is full of thanks that I can participate in understanding and learning from Jung's spiritual journey.

Jung uses a phrase that I share here because it means so much to me. He asks during an inner discussion, "Do we serve the spirit of the times or do we serve the spirit of the depths?" He met this struggle and understood the way to go.

When I entered the world of Jung and analysis, I was 23 and newly married. Reading Jung's words now, in my eighth decade, makes it clear to me that as a young person I served the spirit of the times and not my deepest self. That seems to be the way of the young, but something beckoned inside and I found a way to reach that deeper part of myself.

BIBLIOGRAPHY

Adler, Gerhard. "Personal Encounters with Jung," *Dynamics of the Psyche*. London: Coventure Ltd., 1979.

Alexander, Eben. *Proof of Heaven*. New York: Simon & Schuster, 2009.

Bellow, Saul. *Henderson the Rain King*. New York: Fawcett, 1958.

Blofeld, John. *Bodhisattva of Compassion: The Mystical Tradition of Kuan Yin*. Boulder, CO: Shambhala, 1978.

Clerk, N.W. *A Year with C.S. Lewis*. New York: HarperCollins, 2003.

Dalai Lama, the XIVth. *The Opening of the Wisdom Eye*. Wheaton, IL: Theosophical Publishing House, 1981.

Dallet, Janet. "Active Imagination in Practice," In *Jungian Analysis*. (Murray Stein, Ed.). La Salle, IL: Open Court, 1982 173-191.

de Vries, Ad. *Dictionary of Symbols and Imagery*. Amsterdam: North-Holland Publishing Company, 1974.

Feifel, Herman. *The Meaning of Death*. New York: McGraw-Hill, 1959.

Foy, Glenn. "On Feeling: The Feeling Function Revisited." Paper presented at the 13th Biennial Bruno Klopfer Workshop, Asilomar, CA, 1983.

Frantz, Gilda. "Are We All Widows?" Paper presented at Knowing Woman Conference, C.G. Jung Institute of Los Angeles, 1980b.

_____. "Being Ageless: The Very Soul of Beauty," *Psychological Perspectives* 50(1), 2007. Reprinted with permission of the C.G. Jung Institute of Los Angeles.

_____."Birth's Cruel Secret: O I Am My Own Lost Mother to My Own Sad Child," *Chiron: A Review of Jungian Analysis: Abandonment* (1985). Reprinted with permission of Chiron Publications.

_____."Body and Soul," *Psychological Perspectives* 42(1), 2001. Reprinted with permission of the C.G. Jung Institute of Los Angeles.

_____. "Carrying the Opposites within Oneself: A Book Review," *The San Francisco Jung Institute Library Journal* 18(2), 1999. Reprinted with permission of the C.G. Jung Institute of San Francisco.

_____. "Creativity and Inspiration: An Interview with Stephen Martin," *Psychological Perspectives* 53(4), 2010. Reprinted with permission of the C.G. Jung Institute of Los Angeles.

_____. "Dreams and Sudden Death," in *The Dream and Its Amplification*, (Erel Shalit and Nancy Swift Furlotti, Eds.). 2013, Carmel, CA: Fisher King Press.

_____. "Growing up Poor in Los Angeles: A Memoir," *Psychological Perspectives* 48(1), 2005. Reprinted with permission of the C.G. Jung Institute of Los Angeles.

_____. "I'll See You in My Dreams," Paper presented at the National Conference of Jungian Analysts, Lake Tahoe, Nevada, October 1994.

_____. "Images and Imagination: Wounding and Healing." Paper presented at the C.G. Jung Institute of San Francisco, 1980a.

_____. "Jung, Aging, and Individuation," *Psychological Perspectives* 56(2), 2013. Reprinted with permission of the C.G. Jung Institute of Los Angeles.

_____. "On the Meaning of Loneliness," in *Chaos to Eros*, (Russell Lockhart, Ed.). Los Angeles: C.G. Jung Institute of Los Angeles, 1977.

_____. "Redemption," *Psychological Perspectives* 51(1), 2008. Reprinted with permission of the C.G. Jung Institute of Los Angeles.

_____. "Reflections on Disenfranchisement," *Psychological Perspectives* 34, 1996. Reprinted with permission of the C.G. Jung Institute of Los Angeles.

_____. "Relativity and Relationship," *Psychological Perspectives* 54(1), 2011. Reprinted with permission of the C.G. Jung Institute of Los Angeles.

_____. "Shame." Paper presented at the Tenth International Congress of Analytical Psychology, Berlin, Germany, September 2-9, 1986.

_____. "Spiritual Journeys," *Psychological Perspectives* 53(2), 2010. Reprinted with permission of the C.G. Jung Institute of Los Angeles.

_____. "The Greyhound Path to Individuation," in *Marked by Fire: Stories of the Jungian Way*, (Patricia Damery & Naomi Ruth Lowinsky, Eds.). 2012, Carmel, CA: Fisher King Press.

Frantz, Kieffer. *Depression*. Unpublished paper, 1966.

_____. "The Analyst's Own Involvement with the Process and the Patient." *Journal of Analytical Psychology*, 14(2), 1969.

Gordon, Suzanne. *Lonely in America*. New York: Simon & Schuster, 1976.

Harding, M. Esther. *Woman's Mysteries*. Boston, MA: Shambhala, 1935/2001.

_____. *The Value and Meaning of Depression*. New York: Analytical Psychology Club, 1970.

Harrison, Jane Ellen. *Prolegomena to the Study of Greek Religion*. New York: Meridian, 1955.

I Ching. (Richard Wilhelm & Cary F. Baynes, Trans.). Princeton, NJ: Princeton University Press, 1950.

Jensen, Ferne. (Ed.). *C.G. Jung, Emma Jung, and Toni Wolff: A Collection of Remembrances*, San Francisco, CA: Analytical Psychology Club of San Francisco, 1982.

Jung, C.G. *The Collected Works*. (Bollingen Series XX; H. Read, M. Fordham, & G. Adler, Eds.; R. F. C. Hull, Trans.). Princeton, NJ: Princeton University Press, 1953-1979.

_____. "Answer to Job," in *Psychology and Religion, The Collected Works Vol. 11*. Princeton, NJ: Princeton University Press, 1958.

_____. *Children's Dreams: Notes from the Seminar Given in 1936–1940 by C.G. Jung*. (Lorenz Jung and Maria Meyer-Grass, Eds.; Ernst Falzeder. Trans.). Princeton, NJ: Princeton University Press, 2008.

_____. "Commentary on 'The Secret of the Golden Flower,'" in *Alchemical Studies, The Collected Works, Vol. 13*. Princeton, NJ: Princeton University Press, 1967.

_____. "Definitions," in *Psychological Types, The Collected Works Vol. 6*. Princeton, NJ: Princeton University Press, 1971.

_____. "Introduction to the Religious and Psychological Problems of Alchemy," in *Psychology and Alchemy, The Collected Works, Vol. 12*. Princeton, NJ: Princeton University Press, 1953.

_____. *Letters, Vol 1*. (Gerhard Adler & Aniela Jaffé, Eds.). Princeton, NJ: Princeton University Press, 1973.

_____. *Letters, Vol 2*, (Gerhard Adler & Aniela Jaffé, Eds.). Princeton, NJ: Princeton University Press, 1974.

_____. *Memories, Dreams, Reflections*, (Aniela Jaffé, Ed.). New York: Random House, 1961b.

_____. "Mysterium Coniunctionis," in *Mysterium Coniunctionis, The Collected Works, Vol. 14*. Princeton, NJ: Princeton University Press, 1963.

_____. "On Ultimate Things," in *Psychological Reflections,* (Jolande Jacobi, Ed.). New York: Harper, 1943.

_____. "The Development of Personality," in *The Development of Personality, The Collected Works, Vol. 17*. Princeton, NJ: Princeton University Press, 1954.

_____. "The Dual Mother," in *Symbols of Transformation, The Collected Works, Vol. 5*. Princeton, NJ: Princeton University Press, 1956.

_____. "The Problem with Attitude Type," in *Two Essays in Analytical Psychology, The Collected Works, Vol. 7*. Princeton, NJ: Princeton University Press, 1953.

_____. "The Projection of Psychic Content," in *Psychology and Alchemy, The Collected Works, Vol. 12*. Princeton, NJ: Princeton University Press, 1953.

_____. "Psychology and Literature," in *Spirit in Man, Art, and Literature, The Collected Works, Vol. 15*. Princeton, NJ: Princeton University Press, 1966.

_____. "The Psychology of the Child Archetype," in *The Archetypes and the Collective Unconscious, The Collected Works, Vol. 9i*. Princeton, NJ: Princeton University Press, 1969.

_____. *The Red Book*. (Sonu Shamdasani, John Peck, and Mark Kyburz, Eds.; Sonu Shamdasani, Trans.). New York: Norton, 2009.

_____. "The Symbolism of the Mandala," in *Psychology and Alchemy, The Collected Works, Vol. 12*. Princeton, NJ: Princeton University Press, 1953.

_____. "The Theory of Psychoanalysis," in *Freud and Psychoanalyisis, The Collected Works, Vol. 4*. Princeton, NJ: Princeton University Press, 1961a.

_____. "The Transcendent Function," in *The Structure and Dynamics of the Psyche, The Collected Works, Vol. 8*. Princeton, NJ: Princeton University Press, 1970.

_____. "The Type Problem in Classical and Medieval Thought," in *Psychological Types, The Collected Works, Vol. 6*. Princeton, NJ: Princeton University Press, 1971.

Jung, C.G. and Victor White. *The Jung–White Letters*, (Ann Conrad Lammers and Adrian Cunningham, Eds.). New York: Routledge, 2007.

Keefer, Deri G. *Let's Get Committed: First Lesson Sermons for Sundays After Pentecost.* Lima, Ohio: CSS Publishing Company, 2001.

Kirsch, Hilde. "Reveries on Jung." In *Professional Reports* from the Annual Conference of Society of Jungian Analysts of Northern and Southern California. Printed by the C.G. Jung Institute of San Francisco, 1975..

Kreinheder, Albert. *Body and Soul: The Other Side of Illness.* Toronto: Inner City Books, 1991.

Leonard, Linda. *The Wounded Woman.* Chicago: Swallow Press, 1982.

Martin, Stephen and Aryeh Maidenbaum, (Eds.). *Lingering Shadows: Jungians, Freudians and Anti-Semitism.* Boston: Shambhala, 1991.

Matter of Heart [Film] Screenplay by Suzanne Wagner. Directed by Mark Whitney. Los Angeles: C.G. Jung Institute of Los Angeles, 1986.

May, Rollo. *The Courage to Create.* New York: Norton, 1994.

Neumann, Erich. *Art and the Creative Unconscious.* Princeton, NJ: Princeton University Press, 1959.

_____. *The Great Mother.* New York: Pantheon, 1955.

Perry, John. W. *The Far Side of Madness.* Englewood Cliffs, NJ: Prentice-Hall, 1974.

Roscoe, Will. *Changing Ones: Third and Fourth Genders in Native North America.* New York: St. Martin's Press, 1998.

Schwartz-Salant, Nathan. *Narcissism and Character Transformation.* Toronto: Inner City Books, 1982.

Shamdasani, Sonu. *Cult Fictions: C.G. Jung and the Founding of Analytical Psychology.* London: Routledge, 1998.

Shipley, Joseph T. *Dictionary of Word Origins.* Paterson, NJ: Littlefield, Adams & Co., 1967.

Skeat, William W. *Etymological Dictionary of the English Language.* Oxford, UK: Clarendon Press, 1982.

Taylor, Lou. *Mourning Dress: A Costume and Social History.* London: George Allen & Unwin, 1983.

Thoreau, Henry David. *The Writings of Henry David Thoreau: Journal*, (B. Torrey, Ed.). Charleston, SC: Nabu Press, 2012.

Tripp, Edward. *The Meridian Handbook of Classical Mythology.* New York: New American Library, 1970.

Van Voorst, R.E. *The Anthology of World Scriptures.* Belmont, CA: Thomson Higher Education, 2008.

Von Franz, Marie-Louise. *Creation Myths.* Boston: Shambhala, 1972/1995.

_____. *On Dreams and Death.* Boston: Shambhala, 1984.

Wickes, Frances. *The Inner World of Childhood.* New York: Signet, 1968.

Woodman, Marion. "Psyche/Soma Awareness." Unpublished paper presented at Conference of Jungian Analysts in New York, May 3–6, 1984.

PERMISSIONS

Many thanks to all who have directly or indirectly provided permission to quote their works, including:

Psychological Perspectives for granting permission to reprint the following articles in this publication:

"Being Ageless: The Very Soul of Beauty," *Psychological Perspectives* 50(1), 2007.

"Body and Soul," *Psychological Perspectives* 42(1), 2001.

"Creativity and Inspiration: An Interview with Stephen Martin," *Psychological Perspectives* 53(4), 2010.

"Growing up Poor in Los Angeles: A Memoir," *Psychological Perspectives* 48(1), 2005.

"Jung, Aging, and Individuation," *Psychological Perspectives* 56(2), 2013.

"Redemption," *Psychological Perspectives* 51(1), 2008.

"Reflections on Disenfranchisement," *Psychological Perspectives* 34, 1996.

"Relativity and Relationship," *Psychological Perspectives* 54(1), 2011.

"Spiritual Journeys," *Psychological Perspectives* 53(2), 2010.

Chiron Publications for granting permission to reprint the following article in this publication:

"Birth's Cruel Secret: I Am My Own Lost Mother to My Own Sad Child," by Gilda Frantz. *Chiron: A Review of Jungian Analysis: Abandonment*, 1985. pp. 157–172. Chiron Publications. www.chironpublications.com

The San Francisco Jung Journal for granting permission to reprint the following articles in this publication:

Will Roscoe's "Changing Ones: Third and Fourth Genders in Native North America," Reviewed by Gilda Frantz. *The San Francisco Jung Institute Library Journal*: Volume Eighteen, Number 2, 1999. pp 9-19.

"From a Younger Colleague," by Gilda Frantz. *Remembering Elizabeth: Elizabeth Osterman 1910-1998*, edited by Christina Middlebrook, published by the C.G. Jung Institute of San Francisco, 2000. pp. 39-40.

"Carrying the Opposites within Oneself: A Book Review," *The San Francisco Jung Institute Library Journal* 18(2), 1999.

INDEX

ABOUT THE AUTHOR

Gilda Frantz is the co-editor-in-chief of *Psychological Perspectives*, a journal of Jungian thought of interest to anyone in search of self-understanding. She is one of the original editors of this journal, founded in 1970. For three years she served as president of the C.G. Jung Institute in Los Angeles. Mrs. Frantz is a Director Emerita of the board of the Philemon Foundation, having served throughout the publication period of Jung's *Red Book*. She practices in Santa Monica, California.

ABOUT THE ARTIST

Marlene Frantz is an artist, writer, teacher, and Marriage and Family Therapist who is currently in the analyst training program at the C.G. Jung Institute in Los Angeles. Her work is intuitive and uses a variety of materials including torn paper, acrylic paint, and rusted metal. There is often an element of wonder in her pieces. The title of the cover art is: "Looking Out." Marlene lives and works in Topanga, California.

To learn more about Marlene and her work visit:
www.marlenefrantz.com

You might also enjoy reading:

Marked By Fire: Stories of the Jungian Way edited by Patricia Damery & Naomi Ruth Lowinsky, 1ˢᵗ Ed., Trade Paperback, 180pp, Biblio., 2012 — ISBN 978-1-926715-68-1

The Dream and Its Amplification edited by Erel Shalit & Nancy Swift Furlotti, 1ˢᵗ Ed., Trade Paperback, 180pp, Biblio., 2013 — ISBN 978-1-926715-89-6

Shared Realities: Participation Mystique and Beyond edited by Mark Windborn, 1ˢᵗ Ed., Trade Paperback, 270pp, Index, Biblio., 2014 — ISBN 978-1-77169-009-6

Pierre Teilhard de Chardin and C.G. Jung: Side by Side edited by Fred Gustafson, 1ˢᵗ Ed., Trade Paperback, 270pp, Index, Biblio., 2014 — ISBN 978-1-77169-014-0

Re-Imagining Mary: A Journey Through Art to the Feminine Self by Mariann Burke, 1ˢᵗ Ed., Trade Paperback, 180pp, Index, Biblio., 2009 — ISBN 978-0-9810344-1-6

Advent and Psychic Birth by Mariann Burke, Revised Ed., Trade Paperback, 170pp, 2014 — ISBN 978-1-926715-99-5

Transforming Body and Soul by Steven Galipeau, Rev. Ed., Trade Paperback, 180pp, Index, Biblio., 2011 — ISBN 978-1-926715-62-9

Lifting the Veil: Revealing the Other Side by Fred Gustafson & Jane Kamerling, 1ˢᵗ Ed, Paperback, 170pp, Biblio., 2012 — ISBN 978-1-926715-75-9

Resurrecting the Unicorn: Masculinity in the 21ˢᵗ Century by Bud Harris, Rev. Ed., Trade Paperback, 300pp, Index, Biblio., 2009 — ISBN 978-0-9810344-0-9

The Father Quest: Rediscovering an Elemental Force by Bud Harris, Reprint, Trade Paperback, 180pp, Index, Biblio., 2009 — ISBN 978-0-9810344-9-2

Like Gold Through Fire: The Transforming Power of Suffering by Massimilla & Bud Harris, Reprint, Trade Paperback, 150pp, Index, Biblio., 2009 — ISBN 978-0-9810344-5-4

The Art of Love: The Craft of Relationship by Massimilla and Bud Harris, 1st Ed. Trade Paperback, 150pp, 2010 — ISBN 978-1-926715-02-5

Divine Madness: Archetypes of Romantic Love by John R. Haule, Rev. Ed., Trade Paperback, 282pp, Index, Biblio., 2010 — ISBN 978-1-926715-04-9

Tantra and Erotic Trance in 2 volumes by John R. Haule

> *Volume 1 - Outer Work,* 1st Ed. Trade Paperback, 215pp, Index, Bibligrapy, 2012 — ISBN 978-0-9776076-8-6

> *Volume 2 - Inner Work,* 1st Ed. Trade Paperback, 215pp, Index, Bibligrapy, 2012 — ISBN 978-0-9776076-9-3

Eros and the Shattering Gaze: Transcending Narcissism
by Ken Kimmel, 1ˢᵗ Ed., Trade Paperback, 310pp, Index, Biblio., 2011 — ISBN 978-1-926715-49-0

The Sister From Below: When the Muse Gets Her Way
by Naomi Ruth Lowinsky, 1ˢᵗ Ed., Trade Paperback, 248pp, Index, Biblio., 2009 — ISBN 978-0-9810344-2-3

The Motherline: Every Woman's Journey to find her Female Roots
by Naomi Ruth Lowinsky, Reprint, Trade Paperback, 252pp, Index, Biblio., 2009 — ISBN 978-0-9810344-6-1

The Dairy Farmer's Guide to the Universe in 4 volumes
by Dennis L. Merritt:

> *Volume 1 - Jung and Ecopsychology,* 1ˢᵗ Ed., Trade Paperback, 242pp, Index, Biblio., 2011 — ISBN 978-1-926715-42-1

> *Volume 2 - The Cry of Merlin: Jung the Prototypical Ecopsychologist,* 1ˢᵗ Ed., Trade Paperback, 204pp, Index, Biblio., 2012 — ISBN 978-1-926715-43-8

> *Volume 3 - Hermes, Ecopsychology, and Complexity Theory,* 1ˢᵗ Ed., Trade Paperback, 228pp, Index, Biblio., 2012 — ISBN 978-1-926715-44-5

> *Volume 4 - Land, Weather, Seasons, Insects: An Archetypal View,* 1ˢᵗ Ed., Trade Paperback, 134pp, Index, Biblio., 2012 — ISBN 978-1-926715-45-2

Four Eternal Women: Toni Wolff Revisited—A Study In Opposites
by Mary Dian Molton & Lucy Anne Sikes, 1ˢᵗ Ed., 320pp, Index, Biblio., 2011 — ISBN 978-1-926715-31-5

Becoming: An Introduction to Jung's Concept of Individuation
by Deldon Anne McNeely, 1ˢᵗ Ed., Trade Paperback, 230pp, Index, Biblio., 2010 — ISBN 978-1-926715-12-4

Animus Aeternus: Exploring the Inner Masculine by Deldon Anne McNeely, Reprint, Trade Paperback, 196pp, Index, Biblio., 2011 — ISBN 978-1-926715-37-7

Mercury Rising: Women, Evil, and the Trickster Gods
by Deldon Anne McNeely, Revised, Trade Paperback, 200pp, Index, Biblio., 2011 — ISBN 978-1-926715-54-4

Gathering the Light: A Jungian View of Meditation
by V. Walter Odajnyk, Revised Ed., Trade Paperback, 264pp, Index, Biblio.,
2011 — ISBN 978-1-926715-55-1

The Promiscuity Papers
by Matjaz Regovec, 1ˢᵗ Ed., Trade Paperback, 86pp, Index, Biblio., 2011
— ISBN 978-1-926715-38-4

Enemy, Cripple, Beggar: Shadows in the Hero's Path
by Erel Shalit, 1ˢᵗ Ed., Trade Paperback, 248pp, Index, Biblio., 2008
— ISBN 978-0-9776076-7-9

The Cycle of Life: Themes and Tales of the Journey
by Erel Shalit, 1ˢᵗ Ed., Trade Paperback, 210pp, Index, Biblio., 2011
— ISBN 978-1-926715-50-6

The Hero and His Shadow
by Erel Shalit, Revised Ed., Trade Paperback, 208pp, Index, Biblio., 2012
— ISBN 978-1-926715-69-8

Riting Myth, Mythic Writing: Plotting Your Personal Story
by Dennis Patrick Slattery, Trade Paperback, 220 pp. Biblio., 2012
— ISBN 978-1-926715-77-3

The Guilt Cure
by Nancy Carter Pennington & Lawrence H. Staples, 1ˢᵗ Ed., Trade
Paperback, 200pp, Index, Biblio., 2011 — ISBN 978-1-926715-53-7

Guilt with a Twist: The Promethean Way
by Lawrence Staples,1ˢᵗ Ed., Trade Paperback, 256pp, Index, Biblio., 2008
— ISBN 978-0-9776076-4-8

The Creative Soul: Art and the Quest for Wholeness
by Lawrence Staples, 1ˢᵗ Ed., Trade Paperback, 100pp, Index, Biblio., 2009
— ISBN 978-0-9810344-4-7

Deep Blues: Human Soundscapes for the Archetypal Journey
by Mark Winborn, 1ˢᵗ Ed., Trade Paperback, 130pp, Index, Biblio., 2011
— ISBN 978-1-926715-52-0

Phone Orders Welcomed
Credit Cards Accepted
In Canada & the U.S. call 1-800-228-9316
International call +1-831-238-7799
www.fisherkingpress.com